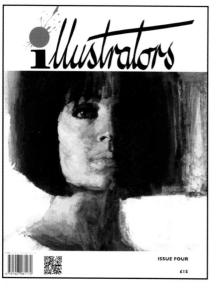

Cover Image: Michael Johnson

ISSUE FOUR
£15

illustrators

The Book Palace
Jubilee House
Bedwardine Road
Crystal Palace
London SE19 3AP

Email: IQ@bookpalace.com
Web: www.bookpalace.com
Contact GW: gw@bookpalace.com
Tel: 020 8768 0022
(From overseas +44 20 8768 0022)
Publisher: Geoff West
Editor & Art Director: Peter Richardson
Associate Editor & Designer: Bryn Havord
Consultant Editor: David Ashford
Featured Writers: Bryn Havord, Jeremy Briggs,
Johnny Mains and Peter Richardson
Subscriptions & Distribution: David Howarth
Online edition: Paul Tanner
Advertising: ads@bookpalace.com
illustratorsquarterly.com

illustrators ISBN 978-1-907081-11-8
ISSN 2052-6520
Issue Number Four Published Summer 2013
Copyright © 2013 by The Book Palace Ltd.

illustrators is published quarterly.
Subscriptions for four issues:
£55 post free UK
£77 airmail Europe
£89 airmail USA/Rest of world

Available in the USA from **budplant.com**
Trade Orders: IQ@bookpalace.com
magazines@centralbooks.com

Printed in China by Prolong Press Ltd

CONTENTS

EDITORIAL

THIS LATEST ISSUE of *illustrators* has a definite sixties feel to it, starting with the boldly bravura painting of one of the premier talents of the era. Michael Johnson's work, with it's emblematic design, and powerful use of paint seemed not only at one with the times, but also to embody the visceral energy of an era where youth and vitality were in an ascendancy, which now seems all the more remarkable with the passing of time. We are very fortunate to have been able to secure the talents of both Mike, and his one time art director and friend, Bryn Havord to bring this feature to life.

Another unique and restlessly inventive artist, whose work first came to prominence in those heady days, is the illustrator Chris McEwan. His eclectic tastes have informed some of the most remarkable, and captivating artwork ever to be seen in print. Chris' work has appeared across a wide variety of media, and his enthusiasm and energy still continues to provide dazzling solutions to the most prosaic of briefs. It was my privilege to be able to chat with Chris about his work and career, and the resultant interview is presented here with some superb examples of his work spanning the decades.

Rounding out the issue, Jeremy Briggs and yours truly take a look at the fascinating world of cutaway artist extraordinaire Leslie Ashwell Wood,. While your senses are still spinning, Johnny Mains will drive a stake into your quivering heart as he opens the door to his mausoleum, and shares with you the story of the artists who added several layers of grue to the covers of the *Pan Book of Horror Stories,* one of the UK's most notorious paperback series.

Added to which, a look at the story behind one of Walter Wyles (soon to be featured in *illustrators*) most memorable illustrations, plus a page of book reviews and your responses to issue 2 of *illustrators,* all go to making this one of our most engrossing issues to date – we hope you enjoy reading it as much as we have in bringing the whole thing together for you.

Michael Johnson

Bryn Havord looks at one of Swinging London's foremost illustrators whose work epitomized the look of the times.

AT MIDNIGHT ON THE 31st of December 1959, we all sang Auld Lang Syne, and said goodbye to the lingering austerity of the post Second World War period. We were suddenly in the "Swinging Sixties"; at least we were in London, which saw the dawn of a new consumerism. It wasn't long before Mr. Harold MacMillan, the British prime minister, was telling us "You've never had it so good!"

Woman magazine, which under the brilliant editorship of Mary Grieve, and with George (Tiny) Watts as art editor, was the world's greatest-selling weekly magazine for women, with weekly sales of 3.5million copies. Grieve swiftly reacted to the social changes that were taking place, and skillfully

 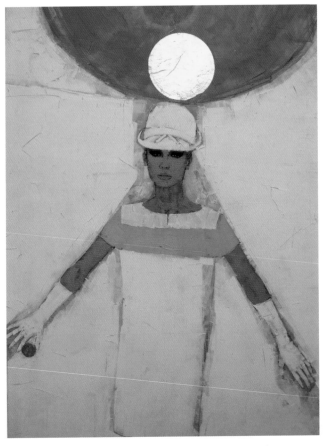

ABOVE & FACING PAGE: Fashion illustrations painted for Willie Landels the editor of *Harpers & Queen* magazine.

ABOVE TOP: Illustration for *Woman* magazine. The model for this painting was our friend Nancy Egerton.
ABOVE: Illustration for a *Sphere* book cover with model Maggie Lorraine.

introduced subtle changes in editorial policy to reflect the new aspirations of the readers. Women's magazine illustration was at its height at this time, and many of the paintings depicted happy couples blissfully enjoying life in their new found stylish homes and social settings. Romantic fiction illustration at its best!

I first met Michael Johnson when I was working as assistant art editor of *Woman* magazine, and he was one of our major contributing illustrators. We both had an interest in fast cars, and by 1962 we both owned 3.8 litre Mark II Jaguars. Johnson was braver than me, and used his Jaguar to tow his Lotus on a trailer to race meetings. He won twelve races, came second in two more, and third in another: a career as a racing driver beckoned. Fortunately for art directors, and the readers of women's magazines and paperback books, the appeal of being an illustrator was the eventual winner.

Johnson was born in Thirsk, a horse-racing town, in the north of England. As a small boy, he liked painting and drawing, but especially liked modeling 3D objects; this later developed into an interest in sculpture, which also beckoned as a possible career. However, he didn't think there was any money in it, and that working as an illustrator promised to be more lucrative. Once again the appeal of illustration was the winner. I thought that some of his work in the mid-sixties, which I also thought was some of his most successful, had a sculptured look about it, as if he had picked up a hammer and chisel, instead of a paintbrush and paint.

In his early teens he started to build model gliders, and learned about aerodynamics; an interest which later led to working with Sir Norman Foster on a book entitled *Aeroplane,* as well as producing several books about gliders. He was also commissioned to make two paintings of

ABOVE: Illustration for
a *Hodder and Stoughton* book cover.
The model was Maggie Lorraine.

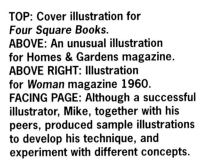

TOP: Cover illustration for
Four Square Books.
ABOVE: An unusual illustration
for Homes & Gardens magazine.
ABOVE RIGHT: Illustration
for *Woman* magazine 1960.
FACING PAGE: Although a successful
illustrator, Mike, together with his
peers, produced sample illustrations
to develop his technique, and
experiment with different concepts.

Boeing 747 aircraft flying over specific landscapes for the Russian airline Transaero, and one of his aeronautical paintings hangs in the entry hall of the Air Force museum in Riyadh, Saudi Arabia.

As a schoolboy Johnson was also a keen racing cyclist, and came third in the North Yorkshire/ South Durham Junior Sprint Championships. When he was sixteen, and a pupil at Thirsk Grammar School, he was awarded an Art Scholarship for three years, to study painting, sculpture, graphic design, and architecture. When he completed the course, his first job was with a design group operating from Leeds in West Yorkshire, where he produced designs and illustrations for a variety of advertising accounts.

His ambition was to break into the international illustration world, and

© IPC Media

Text continues on page 16

ABOVE: Moody use of a restricted palette by Johnson for 'Return to Glenshael', published in *Woman* magazine in 1965.
FACING PAGE: Another book cover for Hodder and Stoughton. The male model for this painting was our friend, the illustrator Renato Fratini (see *illustrators* issue 2).

a year later he went to London and worked for Carlton Artists, which was run on the same lines as the famous Charles E. Cooper Studios in New York City. Carlton Artists specialized in design, illustration and photography, and was the largest studio in Europe.

A year later he was introduced to Joan Farmer, who was setting up as an artists' agent, and she asked Johnson if she could represent him. She introduced his work to all the leading magazines, as well as getting him advertising commissions; one of which was working on the Kellogg account. The ubiquitous red London double-decker buses were covered with his paintings, attempting to entice the citizens of the capital to partake of Kellogg's Sunshine Breakfasts. The same agency handled the Courtaulds account, and he was commissioned to illustrate a series of advertisements by

An Illustration commissioned
in 1965, but not published until the
early seventies. Art directors
commissioned general illustrations
that would fit more or less
any story, and kept them as
back-up stock in case of last minute
emergencies, such as repagination
of the publication to
accommodate changes in the
advertisement content.

ABOVE: A painting published
in *Homes and Gardens*; another
good example of Johnson's
sculpted look.
FACING PAGE: Monochrome
illustration for *Woman's Journal*.

ABOVE: Monochrome illustration for *Woman's Journal* with generous allowance for text to flow around the artwork.
RIGHT: Another illustration for *Woman's Journal* with clever use of the door frame to facilitate a sense of location without losing text space.
FACING PAGE: A strong layout and lighting with Johnson's characteristically vigorous application of paint well to the fore in this *Woman's Journal* spread,

ABOVE: The second part of a ten part serial that I commissioned when I was art director of *Woman's Mirror.* Unfortunately the full-colour opening spread has disappeared. This illustration shows Johnson's skill in leaving well considered space for the placing of type. The main model was Nancy Egerton.

FACING PAGE: The third part of the *Woman's Mirror* serial. I thought that these were the best monochrome illustrations that Johnson had ever produced. They had a nicely sculptured look, as if he had picked up a chisel, instead of a paintbrush. A technique which epitomized much of his work at this time.

Text continued from page 8

the art director Willie Landels, who later became the editor of *Harpers & Queen* magazine. On the fashion front there were the French designers who had a huge influence on British design, including Courrèges and Givenchy with their geometric designs, and Yves Saint Laurent with his "Mondrian" day dress, produced in the autumn of 1965. In London, the Welsh designer Mary Quant was blazing a trail on the fashion front, and Vidal Sassoon designed hairstyles to reflect and compliment the fashions with his geometric haircuts. Johnson's work epitomized the look more than any other illustrator working at that time, and it never ceased to excite me. He lived in London, and had a studio in his flat in Chelsea, and with its white walls and modern furniture, it was very much in the mood of the times.

When I was art director of *Woman's Mirror* in the mid-sixties, he and I worked on many projects together. I would read the stories; decide with the editor where the weekly breaks would come, tell him what they were, and what space he would get for each installment. I never asked to see roughs for two reasons: he was talented enough to make the decisions as to what would be suitable; and selfishly, I looked forward to being

ABOVE: Full page illustration for
Homes and Gardens **magazine.**
FACING PAGE TOP: During the 1960s,
Johnson was producing a lot of work,
which was three dimensional, as well
as the usual two-dimensional paintings.
The publisher of this illustration
is unknown, but it was probably
The Sunday Telegraph Magazine.
FACING PAGE BOTTOM:
Another 2 and 3D combination
painted for a *Penguin* **book cover.**

surprised, and fortunately always delighted, with what he produced.

I thought Johnson had an enormous talent, and found it particularly interesting one day when I went to collect him for a lunch date, and he allowed me to watch him paint an illustration for *Reader's Digest* magazine. It was a painting of an air hostess, as cabin crew were then known. He usually worked from photographic reference, doing the under-painting in quick drying acrylic paint, often scumbling dark colour over light, or more often, light colour over dark. He sometimes finished his paintings in oil colour, with which he could achieve more subtlety. What I especially liked about Johnson's work, was how he usually avoided painting complete backgrounds, but used various situations from the story, or separate elements from a background, to create a montage which, with his outstanding colour sense, was really dramatic. His design of the illustrations always left me

with plenty of choices when it came to positioning the type on the pages. Johnson had tremendous energy, and always had great faith in his own ability. However, despite being one of the most successful illustrators at the time, he felt the need to create new markets for himself, and prepared experimental work on a speculative basis. Usually the specimens showed different compositional approaches, but once again his interest in sculpture influenced what he was doing, and he started producing illustrations and private portrait commissions, using a combination of two-dimensional and three-dimensional works. His illustrations for the covers of the Penguin's Monica Dickens series, and Coronet's The Toff series used a combination of these techniques.

The use of illustrators such as Johnson to produce illustrations for the poster market was a popular trend, and his painting of Carolyn for Frost

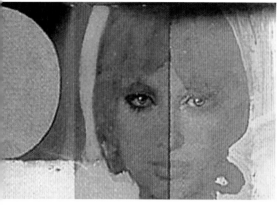

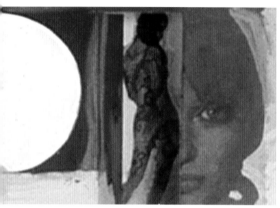

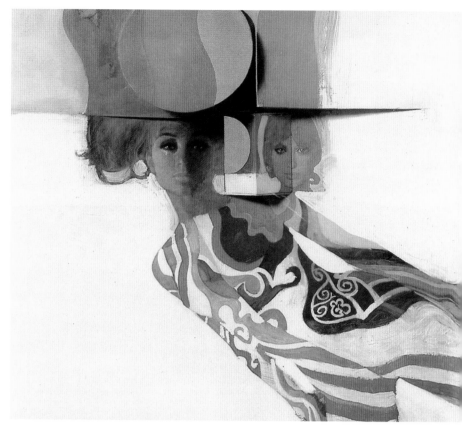

ABOVE: This painting was produced as a print entitled 'Carolyn' by Frost and Reed. It was another 2 and 3D combination, with the top panels extending forward from the main 2D image, and the centre-piece next to Carolyn's head rotated to show separate images.
FACING PAGE: Full page illustration for *Woman's Own*.

and Reed was another two and three-dimensional combination, with the top panels extending forward from the main two-dimensional image, and the centre-piece next to Carolyn's head rotating to show separate images. The British *Woman* and *Woman's Own* magazines, as well as *McCalls* published in America, used his illustrations employing these techniques.

He was never overly impressed or influenced by the work of others, although he was always generous in his praise of what they were doing, if it was good, painterly, and out of the ordinary. He especially liked the work of American illustrators Howard Pyle and Robert Weaver, as he thought they could really paint, and was impressed by Bernie Fuchs' audacity and inventiveness.

We were friendly with the illustrator Renato Fratini, who was godfather to Johnson's daughter Rebecca. Fratini lived in London, and worked in a Victorian purpose-built studio in Kensington with a group of other illustrators, who were mainly Italians. When we met up, we all had a lot of fun, and they all modeled for each other if the clients were too mean to pay for professional models. Restaurant designer, and cartoonist, Enzo Apicella, was one of the ex-pat group, and he helped to change the London scene by transforming the look of Italian restaurants. He replaced the stereotypical raffia covered Chianti bottles and plastic-grapevines, with tiled floors, white walls, abstract art, subtle lighting, and the biggest pepper mills you've ever seen!

The early to mid-sixties had been a period of exciting artistic experimentation for many of the illustrators. From the start to the middle of the decade, I found every working day charged with excitement. Not only with the design work I was doing; but with the work I was commissioning

Text continues on page 38

ABOVE: In this illustration the
shapes above the couple in the clinch
were a box and panel made of
polished aluminum, which were then
painted on. The circular shape
on the left was also a 3D structure.
RIGHT: Double page spread
for *Woman's Own*.
FACING PAGE: Double page spreads
for *Woman's Own*.

ABOVE: A double portrait of the
writer James Joyce painted
for Hodder and Stoughton.
RIGHT: Mike Johnson's recollection
of this painting; "This is one of several
paintings offered to restaurateur
Walter Marity. Every time we ate at his
Meridiana Restaurant, I would sign
the bill, which would then be deducted
from the previously agreed price. This
arrangement would continue until
the painting was paid for. Then we would
start again with another painting.
The impressionist painters in Paris did
the same thing. Eating out was easy;
it was a nice swap, and we got
very good deals, in one of the smartest
restaurants in town."
FACING PAGE: A single page illustration
for *Homes and Gardens* magazine.

TOP: Single page illustration for
The Sunday Telegraph Magazine.
ABOVE: Illustration with Mike and his wife Rosie
shown in the camera lens, and other characters
modeled by friends. From left to right:
Enzo Apicella, restaurant designer and cartoonist,
Walter Maritti, Roy Pegram, in the camera lens
Rosie and Mike. Bottom line Avril Pegram,
Adriana and Gianetto di Coppola.
FACING PAGE: In the mid-sixties posters
reproduced from illustrations were very popular.
The illustration right, a portrait of the
model Jane Lumb, was made for Frost & Reed,
one of the leading poster publishers.

michael johnson

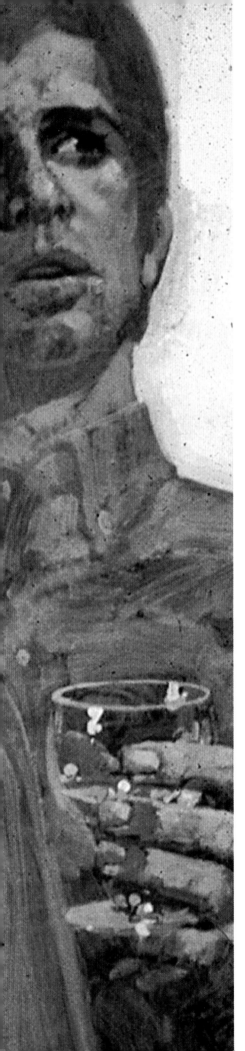

© IPC Media

ABOVE: Joy Hannington, the art director of *Homes and Gardens*, had an intuitive feel and appreciation of illustration typified by these two examples of Johnson's work.
Her approach to bringing out artists' best work was to encourage them to bring their own ideas to an assignment rather than to micro-manage each commission.
LEFT: A detail of a double page spread for *Homes and Gardens* magazine. The male models for this painting were photographer Enzo Ragazzini left, and fellow illustrator Renato Fratini right.

FACING PAGE TOP: Double page
spread for *Woman's Own*.
FACING PAGE BOTTOM: Painting
for *Car And Driver* magazine published
in the USA.
TOP: Penguin Book Cover.
ABOVE: Published as a poster by
a subsidiary of Prints for Pleasure. The brief
was "James Bond girl with gun".
LEFT: Painting for a private commission.

ABOVE: An intriguing use of double images of the main characters, and the treatment of the nude adding a dream-like quality.
FACING PAGE: One of my favourites: a beautiful woman for a stunning private portrait commission.

Illustration Art Gallery Original British & European Illustration Art
www.iartg.com John Millar Watt: Anne Boleyn At Traitor's Gate

TOP LEFT: An illustration for
the German *Stern* Magazine. Fellow
illustrator Renato Fratini is shown
trying to violate the model Sue Longhurst,
and Mike's stepson Mark is the boy
picking up the dagger in the foreground.
Mike said, "Renato and Sue seemed
to be enjoying their work,"
BELOW LEFT: Double page spread
for *Woman's Own*. Another
2 and 3D painting.
THIS PAGE: Cover for Corgi Books.
The model was Sue Longhurst.

Monica Dickens
Flowers
on the Grass

Monica Dickens
Thursday
Afternoons

A selection of book covers, including those for *Penguin's* Monica Dickens novels in 1969, and for John Creasey's The Toff series; for these Johnson used a combination of 2D and 3D techniques. The covers for novels by Dorothy Eden and Hermina Black published by *Coronet* were two dimensional.

Monica Dickens
One Pair of Hands

Monica Dickens
My Turn to
Make the Tea

DOROTHY EDEN
author of NEVER CALL IT LOVING
WHISTLE FOR THE CROWS

THE STORY OF A BEAUTIFUL GIRL
WHOSE SEARCHINGS FOR THE
TRUTH OF THE PRESENT THREW HER
HEADLONG INTO THE MYSTERIES
OF THE PAST.

from the author of MELBURY SQUARE
Dorothy Eden
Samantha

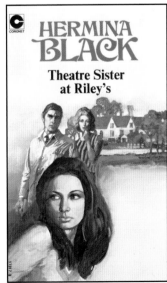

HERMINA BLACK
Theatre Sister
at Riley's

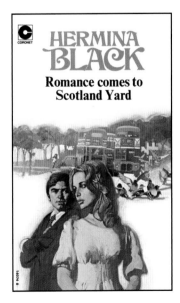

HERMINA BLACK
Romance comes to
Scotland Yard

Clarence
kissed her
tenderly,
took his bowler hat
and stalked
across the gangway
for town.
"Rosie,
I do this for you,"
he said.
Appalling
but true,
she knew,
for each
scheming trip
was essential to
OPERATION
ROSEBUD
a warm and
humorous
story about
the many sides
of love
and honor,
by the
master storyteller
Sean O'Faolain

Rosebud met him one summer afternoon in London while she was lying flat on her face on the pavement of St. James's Street outside Prunier's restaurant during an air raid. "Suited him down to the ground," she used to say long afterward with a laugh. "I ILLUSTRATED BY MICHAEL JOHNSON. COPYRIGHT © 1966 BY SEAN O'FAOLAIN.

didn't stand a chance." When the bomb fell somewhere in Green Park, she looked sideways and saw a handsome young fellow in an R.A.F. uniform lying beside her, head on elbow, pensively admiring her. He might well admire her—hair like a wheatfield

in September; two big, frightened eyes of cornflower blue; aged, he rightly guessed, about nineteen, and nicely fat. Plump girls were at a premium in London during those years of food rationing. She was happy to let him lead her off to the Ritz for a drink

downstairs in the crowded bar, all present, he assured her, being either spies or counterspies, heros or prostitutes. He told her that he was in Intelligence, with the effective rank of wing commander, and that his father owned *(Continued on following page)* 59

Text continued from page 20

from British artists, and with the work available from the American illustrators. Going into W. H. Smith, the main news agents and paperback book sellers at the time, was a must every week, as we didn't want to miss any of the terrific work being published in the magazines, on paperback covers, and in newspapers.

However, by the end of the decade magazine readers were starting to disappear. The commercial television companies started to obtain larger portions of the available advertising revenue, and newspaper and magazine page counts went down. In common with the illustrators working in the USA, the illustrators working in the United Kingdom started to feel the pinch. There was a decline in the interest in romantic fiction in women's magazines, and for some reason art directors and art editors started asking the illustrators to produce more highly finished work, which tended to reduce the contrast between the work produced by individual artists, and they increasingly turned to photography instead of painted illustration.

During a trip to New York City in 1965, I showed William Cadge, the art director of *Redbook* magazine, some transparencies of Johnson's work. Cadge had a story about a couple living on a houseboat in London, and he immediately commissioned Johnson to paint the illustration for the story. In 1969, Johnson went to live in the USA, and on the strength of the work he had done for *Redbook,* he obtained work from *McCall's, Cosmopolitan, Woman's Day* and *Sports Illustrated.*

The 1970s proved to be a challenging decade for every illustrator in Britain trying to pursue a career in magazine illustration. Work became harder to find on both sides of the Atlantic, but the market for paperback book cover

TOP: Johnson's first commission for the American *Redbook* magazine in 1965. ABOVE AND FACING PAGE: Book covers for Hodder & Stoughton.

illustration remained fairly buoyant here in the United Kingdom.

In the late sixties and early seventies, Johnson continued to work for magazines and book publishers including Penguin, Pan, Granada, Collins, Fontana, Panther, and *Reader's Digest* in both London and New York. He also won a contract with a German advertising agency in Dűsseldorf, as a consultant art director and illustrator, working on experimental three-dimensional painting and sculpture artworks used in market research. He continued to have his work published as posters by Frost and Reed, Paul Hamlyn, and Scandecor in Sweden.

In a career spanning over fifty years, his work, in addition to illustration for magazines, has encompassed just about every area of the illustrative arts ranging from industrial design, book publishing, painting, and sculpture; including commissions to paint portraits. He has also been involved in aerodynamics, and aircraft and glider design.

In 1975, he went to live in the south of France, where he still lives and works every day. He has become increasingly interested in Arab culture, and conceived the idea for a book of Moroccan cooking, written by Samira Fouhami, which he illustrated, and which includes many traditional recipes from Fez, Marrakech, Meknès, and Essaouira. The book incorporates historical text, and a CD of modern Arab music.

In 2011, Johnson was in Tripoli negotiating with a gallery to hold an exhibition of his paintings with Arab themes and subject matter, when he had to beat a hasty retreat, as the insurgents embarked upon their mission to depose Colonel Muammar Gaddafi.●

● *To see more of Michael's work, go to* **www.michaeljohnson777.com**
A selection of Michael's original illustrations are
available at **www.graphiccollectibles.com**

TOP & ABOVE: Covers for Hodder & Stoughton, painted in the 1970s, showing the much tighter style of painting which was being demanded by the art editors and their marketing departments.
FACING PAGE: Tina Turner painted for a vinyl record sleeve in the 1970s.

Chris McEwan

illustrators editor, Peter Richardson, talks to the artist about the experiences, ideas and influences that helped to shape his perennially inventive, and idiosyncratic illustration.

CM: I grew up in Brighton and by the age of eleven I was at Brighton Art College. They did Saturday morning classes, where I met one or two people who are still in the business. I knew what I wanted to do, and I left school early to pursue my dream, but I ended up returning to school to get the necessary qualifications before becoming a full time student at the age of seventeen. I had my eighteenth birthday party, and I was probably the youngest person ever to attend Brighton Art College as a full time degree course student. By that time I had discovered *Eagle* comics. We were only allowed one comic, and that was it. While I was reading 'The Life of Churchill' ('The Happy Warrior') I was hit round the head with that idea: "Hang-on! somebody's job is to draw this". I didn't know how to do it, but I had words with my excellent art teacher, Geoffrey Lintott, who was supporting me, and he said "Yes, you go to Brighton Art College". So I went full time in 1963 to 1967, and had people like John Lord to support me. You probably know him?

PR: John was my tutor and a real inspiration.

CM: Well, he was wonderful. He gave me an idea of what might be possible.

ABOVE: McEwan's lifelong love affair with robots is evident in these two card and print designs. **FACING PAGE:** A promotional poster for Tony Cuthbert's Animation Studio. Cuthbert, ran a Soho – based animation studio producing work for film and TV for clients both in the UK and internationally.

ABOVE:Chris McEwan photographed in 1981, along with some "friends" for the 1981 exhibition 'Robots' at Brighton Art College.
ABOVE RIGHT: A 1970s illustration for a French advertising agency. McEwan's graphic sensibilities accorded well with French Art Directors, whose appreciation of 'bande dessinée' was way in advance of their UK counterparts.
FACING PAGE: A poster for Roy Turk who was a pioneer of special effects and camera work in the UK animation industry, with a CV that included work on Halas and Batchelor's 1954 release of 'Animal Farm'.

Whilst there, illustrators that I came across, who I still love, include John Hassall, Cecil Aldin, William Nicholson – he used to live up the road from my folks in Rottingdean–Lawson Wood, Charles Robinson, Arthur Rackham, and Edmund Dulac, and I also discovered 'Rupert Bear' which was a real revelation. I had grown up in a house without books, so that surreal other world of 'Rupert Bear' really, made a huge impact on me.

After Brighton I then went to The Royal College of Art (RCA) from 1967-1970, and happily found myself part of a talented group of like-minded people. (It was while I was there that I became aware of Eduardo Paolozzi. He had an exhibition in the Victoria and Albert Museum and it was his love of machines that struck a chord with me and later lead to my use of toys, especially robots, as inspiration for my own work).

The first term I was at the RCA *The Sunday Times* newspaper employed me to do the first full colour illustrated page they had ever featured, which was even mentioned on the TV news!

PR: Fantastic!

CM: Yes, it was amazing. But because it went so well they gave me another page after that. It was all too much, too soon, really. I was working on that, plus lots of editorial illustrations and I was trying to fulfill the demands of the RCA course work as well. Even so it was just an incredible time.

I had always enjoyed costume, so I did a lot of work for the fashion magazines. I wasn't so much concerned with being a fashion illustrator, but certainly that love of costume, and being next-door to the V&A with all its collections was a constant source of inspiration. While I was there Paul Hogarth came along, and I went out drawing with him, and he really instilled that love of drawing, and the love of landscape, and architecture. He told me about the Brandywine Tradition, and I discovered Maxfield Parrish. So finally, when

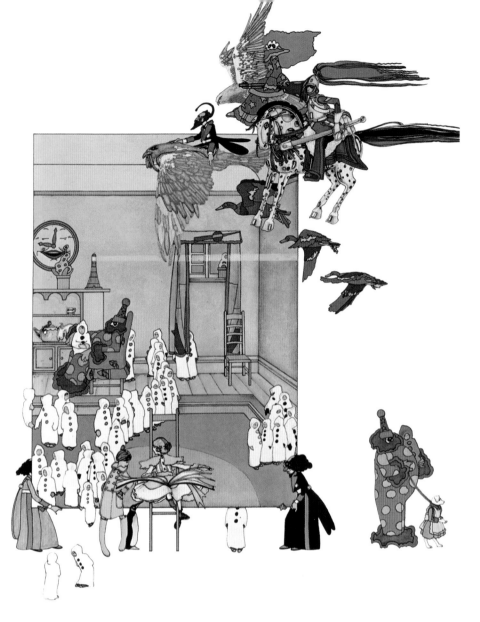

I did go to America, well that's where I headed. I'd also become aware of people like David Hockney who had that graphic sensibility–at last a voice about the here and now. Hockney was about the 20th Century. My work tended to be influenced by Victorian/Edwardian stuff mixed with Pop Art. But there was also so much else happening at the time which I was keen to explore, magazines like *Twen* which featured the work of illustrators such as Heinz Edelmann, who then went on to create the stylings for 'Yellow Submarine' animated feature. 'Yellow Submarine' was in production at the time and I could have also got involved with working on that, but I was just too busy to make the commitment. Many years later, a friend who had an Art Deco shop in Stuttgart with some of my work on the walls, told me that Heinz Edelmann often came into the shop, (he was professor at the local art college), and had recognized my work!

I thought, "How amazing is that!"

And this week they've been celebrating 'Little Nemo' on Google…

PR: Oh, I watched that and thought, I wonder if Chris is enjoying this!

CM: Jean Giraud (aka Moebius), created the stylings for the Japanese animated film of 'Little Nemo' and along with Nemo's creator Winsor McCay, is another huge influence. I didn't really know about 'Little Nemo' until

ABOVE: 'Les Portes', a poster for Bruynzeel, Paris 1970s. At this stage in his career, the artist was creating much of his art, such as this image with flat washes of gouache on illustration board with ink lines added with technical pen, brushes, French curves and rulers.
ABOVE LEFT: An early example of self-promotion, with the artist's love of costume well to the fore.
FACING PAGE: A poster by McEwan for Alpha International Mobilier, created when the artist was based in Paris, reflecting a truly eclectic mix of ideas and influences, but with the distinctive McEwan imprimatur giving it that extra lift.

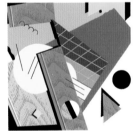

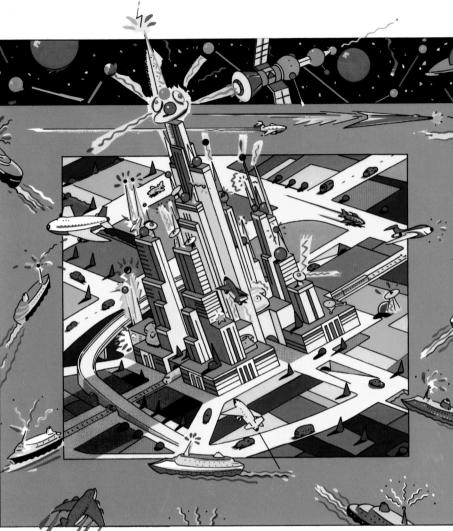

ABOVE TOP: An illustration of the first satellite for British Telecom. As the artist wryly commented; "They had no photographs of the actual thing, so I had to invent it".
ABOVE: Magazine illustrations for Conran reveal the artist's love of Matisse.
ABOVE RIGHT: Another illustration on the theme of telecommunications.
FACING PAGE: 'Spaceship', a typically quirky interpretation of a familiar theme, provided an image for both postcards and posters.

I was asked to go to Paris by my agent as a fashion illustrator and I said, "Oh well yes, I'd love to be in Paris" So I went. I hadn't been there for five minutes when I started doing everything else including animation. But the guys said well your work is so influenced by 'Little Nemo', and I didn't know who they were talking about! So they went off and got me the album, that's why my 'Little Nemo' album is all in French.

PR: Ah right, yes.

CM: Then I discovered Lyonel Feininger ('Wee Willy Winkie'), and then of course George Herriman with 'Krazy Kat'. So I was going from being a penniless art student in London to a penniless illustrator in the middle of Paris, but café society got me into every agency, and every magazine, and I did everything that any illustrator would want to do. It was a wonderful entrée into Europe and I hadn't been there very long when I acquired agents in Amsterdam and Germany, as well as having one in London. I came back to live in Brighton—not London—and was invited to teach at Brighton Art College. And teaching there for one or two days a week remained constant for about the next eighteen years. While there I had my trip to the USA and, of course, I headed straight for Disneyland, soaking up all those influences. While on the East Coast I discovered Rockwell, stayed with friends up in Pennsylvania—got introduced to the work of N.C. Wyeth and the Howard Pyle School of Illustration, which was all a part of the Brandywine Tradition.

I used to walk into Philadelphia and I walked into the buildings where the publishers were, and introduced myself. I suppose I rediscovered architecture; new architecture, and buildings as doughnuts, and diners, and toys again. In Philadelphia, in the fields, they did half a dozen markets, and they guaranteed you a million items—I don't know who counted them to check there were a million items—but there, of course, they had all the robots, and all the toys you could ever wish for, because everybody had come from Europe, and here they were selling the stuff they had brought with them. It was something of a revelation, apart from the fact they were also selling cars and all the rest. I just thought that was completely wonderful. You think of all the reasons you went to America, and there they were! When I got to Los Angeles, I was down there by the Grauman's Chinese Theatre, I remember I bumped into this guy, quite literally, I was staring inside this toy shop window, waiting for it to open so I could get my robots…

PR: (laughter) Needs must!

CM: Must have! Talking about it later, I said to the guys, "I've met another of your weird LA people pretending to be Buffalo Bill", and they said "No! He is! That's his son!" So I felt I'd gone full circle, and I had really done my American thing. I was staying in a group of apartments courtesy of an American friend I just met; one was taking photographs of Muhammad Ali; another one was doing houses for the biggest stars, including Marlon

ABOVE: Design for a diary page on a theme of cocktails. Combining lively graphics with a mix of primary and pastel colours, the artist creates a truly individual response to the brief.

49

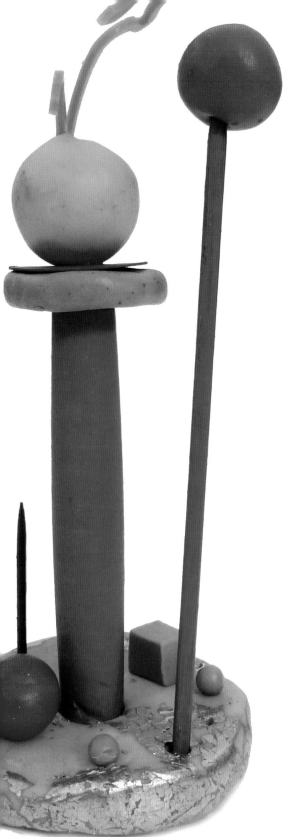

Brando, and the apartment block was put up by the guy who was the newspaper—William Randolph Hearst—the legendary newspaper tycoon. And, what's the most famous film ever made, the most successful?

PR: Oh, um…Citizen Kane, with Orson Welles playing Hearst?

CM: Yes, well, that was him. I found myself in that situation as well. A lot of people don't get on in LA, but we had the most wonderful time. So much later, when I was asked to go and work over there, of course I went. But that was much later. So, at the time I was still living in Brighton and I had been repped by a number of agents in London before I eventually settled with CIA (Central Illustration Agency), which was Brian Grimwood's brainchild. Brian had established himself as an incredibly successful illustrator but was looking for new areas to pour his energies into and I think I was one of the first people he rang up to say, "Do you think this is a good idea?" Eventually I left Brighton to move to Newick to the home that I have in the Sussex countryside. And, of course with Carol (Chris' wife Carol Lawson), who I met at Brighton. It's rather lovely working with another illustrator, because, if I can't draw something, she can. And you can turn to somebody and say, "What's it like?"; and if it's rubbish, she'll tell you. And, hopefully too, if you don't have self-confidence she'll bat you round the head and say "get on with it". That's been a constant source of comfort and interest. Her very particular kind of work and application, and her ability to produce the techniques has always astonished me, so that's been nice to have.

Because of our interest in America, and the way in which my work developed, the influence of all things Japanese, and the whole love of merchandise proved very important. We went to America eventually because we had a radio and TV tour to do based on Carol's work with a big merchandising company in America. So we entered the world of merchandise quite early on. A lot of the comic characters, and the way in which I think, and the books on my shelves, are devoted to that whole area. A lot of creatives collect toys and know where the iconography comes

ABOVE AND FACING PAGE: Examples of Chris McEwan's maquettes reveal, yet again, the artist's playful inventiveness, and love of shape and colour, as he takes his ideas beyond the confines of his sketch books and into the realm of the third dimension.

from, and that leads onto films like 'Toy Story' which are now so familiar. I suppose you would say that my love of Miró, Picasso and Matisse has come full circle, and it's difficult to say how those elements actually find their way into my work, but they do. They have all informed the weird and wonderful drawings in my ideas books which has led to my maquettes and 3d work.

PR: Yes, I found that fascinating, as I hadn't realized that you were working in 3D to quite such an extent. In fact, you sent me an e-mail with a little attachment of a fish, which you had evidently modelled.

CM:Well, it took my students to point out how often fish appeared in my work–they even presented me with one that lights up! After I left teaching at Brighton Art College, I did a few years helping to run the illustration course at Worthing and then I was invited up to Kingston. I devised a programme for drawing and painting for the designers and eventually I got to deal with most of the international students; I became a counsellor for them really. A student from Thailand made a beautiful sketchbook for me but, of course, when you get a book like that, you daren't draw in it. So she said "I want you to fill it up by the end of term, or I'm not giving it to you". (laughter). After that I got back to doing stuff in a book, rather like a diary, a visual diary. And anything I was thinking of, or anything that came up in my mind which spawned a whole series of ideas books. (It has been said that I ought to publish them just as they are). The maquettes evolved from there and not a few owe something to the robot world.

I included both books and maquettes in my last Robot exhibition, alongside my collection of 300 robots, guns and rockets. ('Robot Invasion' at Hove Museum and Gallery in 2011–2012).

Drawing is, for me, a key component of the creative process but there is a question in all teaching establishments, let alone art colleges, about just how much people do actually draw. I think it is really rather lamentable that the basic requirement of drawing has somehow lapsed. I don't want to sound like a dinosaur, but it would be nice if some of that was rediscovered.

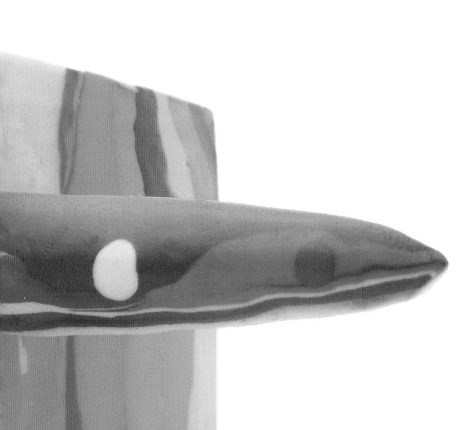

Acccording to McEwan, the catalyst for the maquettes was a sketchbook that one of his students made for him. His initial reluctance to draw inside the beautiful book was soon overcome, when the student insisted that he use it as it was intended.

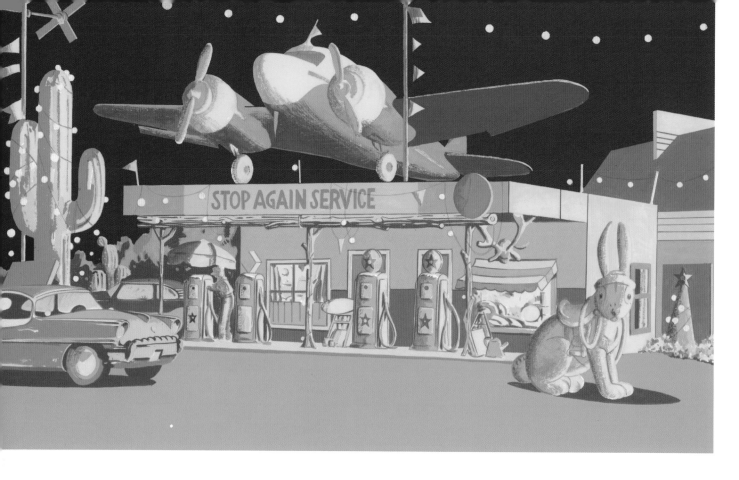

ABOVE: 'Stop Again Service',
artwork for a poster and greetings
card, with the artist's love
of US iconography, Art Deco, and '50s
automobiles well to the fore.
FACING PAGE: "Mayfly", McEwan's
paintings often feature an
exploration of iconography that recur
throughout his work, as in this
delightful example where his rabbits,
olives, and winged insects
provide the springboard for this
delightful calendar illustration.

When I was a student it was an absolutely essential part of the course.

PR: Well my belief has long been that even when I was at art college, we didn't have the kind of disciplined teaching of drawing and anatomy that previous generations had, because it had fallen out of favour. It was optional for you to go to life class, for example. For me, mastery of the figure is at the heart of all drawing.

CM: Well, you would think that was the basic thing wouldn't you? I mean, I know that they opted out...most classes unfortunately went from thirty to sixty, but with the designers it was something like eighty. But if you'd said there's an art class tonight, and you've all got to go, you just don't have the space to fit them all in. So then you say, well it's optional. Actually, recently, just before I left it was oversubscribed; people couldn't wait to get there, they loved it. In some way it's gone full circle, and if you offer it to people, and encourage them of course, and you have a good teacher, they would think it essential as well. It's a nice antidote to all that stuff you have to do with computers, and the discipline, and having no time just to just sit down and draw. So there you are; we've got it off out chests! I know I've made a note of it down here to say, oh yes, RCA, I was there with Quentin Blake, Michael Foreman, and Brian Robb who was the head of the department. But my fellow students were George Hardy and John Pasche who designed the Rolling Stone tongue logo. Among visiting lecturers we particularly asked to see Edward Ardizzone, whose book illustrations, incidentally, had terrified me as a child–and then there he was, an avuncular, tweed-clad old gentleman covered in snuff!

PR. Talking of the RCA in those dim and distant days, I recall you telling me about the access you had to the V&A.

CM: Well, we were in the V&A. We were at the back, and had, what we liked to call, a 'secret door' which led directly into the museum. We used to walk by all this art, including Leonardo's note books, every day. In the first two or three weeks your jaw would drop because you couldn't believe what you were looking at, but in no time at all you got a bit blasé and just wanted a coffee! You more or less took it all for granted, but it was a very cosy place to be.

I actually wrote most of my thesis in the print room, and after a while they used to leave all this reference stuff on the desk for me. This included the most wonderful drawings of costumes from the 1920s and 1930s in Paris. Across

ABOVE TOP: 'Silbury Hill',
the prehistoric chalk mound from
Avebury, Wiltshire provides the
inspiration for a limited edition print
from the 'Sacred Sites' series.
ABOVE: 'Friends', a delightful
juxtaposition of Enid Blyton style
children and a toy robot.
ABOVE RIGHT: 'Village Street'.
McEwan serves up yet another
surreal take on rural landscape for
the Design Council.
FACING PAGE: Fellow Brightonian
illustrator, Aubrey Beardsley makes
a cameo appearance in an illustration
from 'Cecino the Tiny', a story from
Idries Shah's 'World Tales', published
by Allen Lane 1979.

the road was the Natural History Museum, and in those comparatively more relaxed days you could take anything down that you liked, instead of filing for it. The first book I took down was about the illustrator Sydney Parkinson who went with Captain Cook to the other side of the world. The watercolour illustrations were as bright as the day he had done them. And I thought; I like this place!

In addition I also had easy access to the Science Museum which also exerted its influence on me—I had a close encounter one day on my way into the Science Museum for the inevitable and much longed for cup of coffee. Thinking of nothing much beyond the delights of the cafeteria, I pushed aside this rusting heap of hardware and only later realized that it was the space capsule that had taken the astronauts to the moon! But machinery does hold a distinct fascination for me, I didn't fully understand this until the Robot exhibition when someone asked, "Where did you get

ABOVE AND FACING PAGE:
Sketches and working drawings for
the shelved 'Alice in Wonderland' film.
One of McEwan's last commercial
film projects. It was axed when
Tim Burton started work on his own
version of Lewis Carroll's
much loved story.

this love of machines from?" It was Carol who said, "Well, your father was an engineer". Also my grandfather had been an engineer and a designer and my Scottish grandfather was a photographer and so on

PR: Well, that's fascinating because I was going to bring you back to that offhand comment that you made at the start of this interview, when you said you grew up in a house with no books, and not a lot of visual stuff around. Which prompts the question...

CM: Well, yes. I'll tell you briefly what it was: my great-grandfather, Henry Taylor, moved in Royal circles and is now a waxwork up in Warwick Castle. He was secretary to King Edward VII. As much as you can be a friend of a King, he was. And my great-grandmother was Queen Alexandra's sewing maid. He retired to Newmarket where there were horses everywhere, and the King used to come and visit. My great-grandparents eventually divorced and great-grandmother ended up in Rottingdean, down the road from Sir Edward Burne-Jones whose visitors included the likes of William Morris and the other Pre-Raphaelites and whose neighbour was Rudyard Kipling. The story was that as a child my mother's nanny used to sit for John Everett Millais. When the family moved to Brighton it was to a Victorian/Edwardian house full of the clutter that the previous generations had passed down. My grandfather was an artist, and he drew animals in particular including the race-horses that turned up at Newmarket. So in fact the house had an assortment of pictures, and also the beautiful silks from great-uncle Tom Loates, the champion jockey, who rode for the Rothschilds. (One of the

by Whitmore

earliest movie films is of him winning the Derby in 1890). I suppose that's the first inkling I had of costume, these giant Victorian wardrobes full of clothes and shoes. And then there is the connection with Granny and the stories of Buffalo Bill that she would regale us with. (Hence my delight with the Buffalo Bill encounter in Hollywood!). They were touring the world at a time when most people didn't travel. So they brought back cowboy guns and Indian headdresses and filled us with tales of what might be. The family knew that there was something out there; something artistic, that there was another area of life. But after the Second World War, everything changed. There was some acceptance of it, but not a book in sight. Nobody ever went out and bought me a book on art, or thought to buy me art materials. I would draw on anything. Women's magazines had illustrations of fashion and I was very influenced by all of that. My early efforts were all of that kind of subject matter. However, when I was sixteen I went to France and stayed in a wonderful house north-west of Paris that frequently turns up in war movies, because it was the headquarters for the Germans in both world wars. It was a huge house and half of it was rented out, during the summer, to a buyer from Dior. I got talking to him and again it all fell into place. I thought, "Hang on, you mean you actually work for a fashion house?" I wrote a letter saying, "I'm not coming home, I'm going to art college". So all those little strands started to come together. As it was, I had to return to school, of course. I actually attended a school, (which was right opposite my house), that was styled as a copy of a Venetian villa; the architect was Sir

ABOVE: Illustration from 'The Nine Tasks of Mistry', Little Brown 1995. FACING PAGE: One of the artworks from the Italian edition of 'Pinocchio'. Although long out of print, McEwan's version remains one of the most captivating interpretations of this classic tale.

Charles Barry who had designed the Houses of Parliament. Presumably he had just been on his European tour, and halfway between the sea and the Downs he designed this marvellous house, and that was my school. I used to draw it all the time; I suppose it was that love and acknowledgement of architecture, even though I wasn't aware of it then. I took my 'O' Level at twelve and took my 'A' level at fourteen and was back at the Art College to study for a three hour written paper on the History of Architecture. And I guess some of it stayed with me.

PR: You evidently had a fairly full-on exposure to a lot of rich and varied stimuli at an age where all these experiences really do make a very vivid and long-lasting impression.

CM: Well, it was very easy for me. Because I could actually draw, because it was something I could do, and I was increasingly unhappy at school. Once I got to the art class nobody had to force me to do anything. I would wander off and spend hours lost in drawing. Our school was run by Catholic Brothers, and they were beginning to lose me.

I needed something else and the allure of comics, rock'n'roll and long hair was heady stuff. We were not allowed to read comics but with an engineer for a father, the *Eagle*, of course, was opened up to us with those double page spreads where and you could see the workings of the Titanic, or whatever it was...

PR: Oh yes, the cut-away drawings by Leslie Ashwell Wood. (See the feature on Leslie Ashwell Wood on page 76)

CM: You could see why we were allowed the *Eagle*, as my father just wanted to read it as well. So it was an escape for me to get to art college, and once I entered it, I never left!

PR: And you and Carol are still busy now?

CM: Well yes, we didn't want to continue the mad commercial stuff that we'd always done, and we wanted to move sideways, and do other things. After

ABOVE, RIGHT, AND FACING PAGE: More imagery from the Mondadori 'Pinocchio'. Eschewing a more literal approach to illustrating the story, McEwan's artwork used Collodi's text as a springboard for exploring the surreal and fantastic themes that characterise this classic tale.

I had finished teaching, I started painting, to see if I could do that and also do prints and so on. As Carol said: "There's never a right time, so why don't you do it now?" I love the landscape where we live, so that was my starting point. Then we joined Artwave (a Lewes based arts group) and we exhibit our work in that every year. Along the way the 'Robot' exhibition happened, so in between that and the other jobs that have come my way, I am still keeping very busy!

I suppose the last time I actively did the commercial thing was to go to Paris to work on an animated film. It was 'Alice in Wonderland' but unfortunately, as chance would have it, Tim Burton had also decided he would make an Alice film, so it was no contest and ours had to be abandoned.

PR: Oh! I was going to ask you about that. I'd assumed that those drawings were for a book, but they were for the film?

CM: They were for a film! And they said, "Oh well, never mind because we'll do the book", but I haven't pursued it. In fact there is still a certain amount of my work that leans towards publishing, and Carol and I think that it's about time I went back to doing books. I don't have anyone to work with at the moment so it's quite a steep learning curve getting back into that, and presenting my ideas

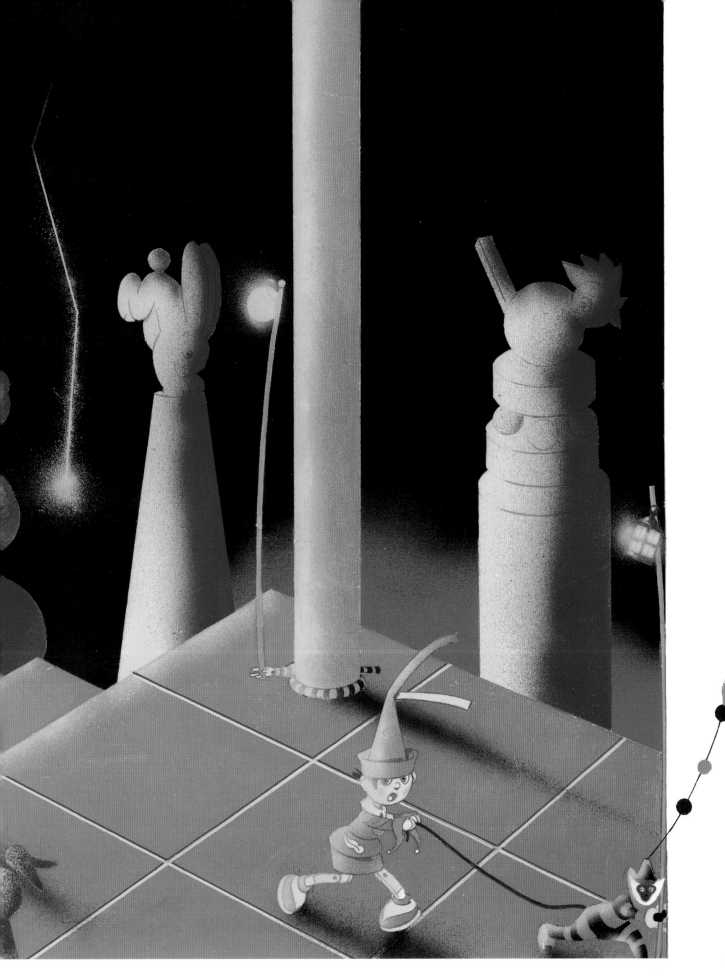

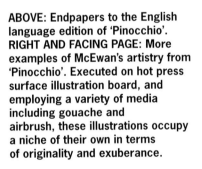

ABOVE: Endpapers to the English language edition of 'Pinocchio'. RIGHT AND FACING PAGE: More examples of McEwan's artistry from 'Pinocchio'. Executed on hot press surface illustration board, and employing a variety of media including gouache and airbrush, these illustrations occupy a niche of their own in terms of originality and exuberance.

again. I am currently working on a robot book to accompany my next robot exhibition at The Lightbox Gallery in Woking later this year and I would like to see the Italian edition of 'Pinocchio' reprinted.

PR: Well yes, because I only ever had one glance at the Italian edition. I've got the English edition, which is quite small but beautiful, but the Italian one is out of this world.

CM: Oh, how kind. Well it was a dream job; when I got the 'phone call asking if I would like to do the commemorative edition. The publisher came over to see me, and I was a little apprehensive because 'Pinocchio' is akin to the Patron Saint of Italy. I thought the Mafia might come and get me! As it turned out, I was set free to do whatever I wanted, without restriction. The only thing they changed was the Blue Fairy. I'd given her blonde hair, which is of course what Disney had done and they wanted it changed to black because it's Italian. They were probably quite right. (But it was not very well done on the front cover).

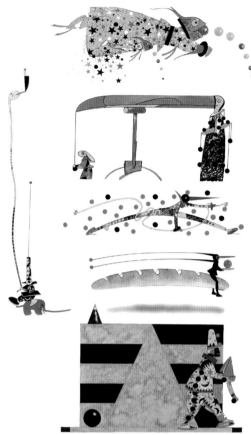

Commissioned on the strength of the work that he created for the earlier (and greatly condensed) award winning nursery edition, the team at Mondadori provided McEwan with a much larger canvas on which to work his magic. The result, though relatively unknown in the UK and US, still ranks as one of the most captivating illustrated children's books to see print in recent years.

PR: Well, I was going to ask you about that, so they executed the change in-house without getting back to you?

CM: Yes–and I think they used a black biro! It was so lovely being able to draw costumed characters with that Italian flavour. Once again it was the coming together of so many things. I won a prize at Bologna for the first book, and the publishers took both of us to Italy, to be wined and dined. And after that, we went on to Venice and so I got my chance to reconnect with Italian architecture. I have very happy memories of working in publishing and I really would like to get back to it as I think a lot of my ideas could work as books.

PR: Yes, because books are lovely. I can remember when I left Brighton Art College, it was always the dream that one would go off and get a publisher, and you'd publish perhaps two books a year, and then you'd do other stuff, you know, by the by. It's just not like that these days.

CM: Well I must say I've got out of the habit of doing it. In the old days you

ABOVE: The artist in his Sussex studio, surrounded by the accumulated iconography of a life dedicated to illustrating the extraordinary.

● *Chris McEwan & Carol Lawson's art can be seen at :*
www.lawsonmcewan.com

turned up to a publisher and you had a working arrangement with them. Nowadays most people find it extremely hard to get their work even seen.

PR: Well Chris, I've written down all these things I wanted to ask, and you've anticipated them all, including ambitions for the future, which I suspect is publishing and prints...

CM: Well yes, we do our own prints at home; we have a wonderful setup with the computers and stuff, so we produce cards and limited edition prints that we show in our exhibitions, as well as originals. We will certainly continue with that and because of my earlier experience with animation, I would love to be involved in that area again. Meanwhile I am pursuing my book ideas and working towards an exhibition themed around the 'War of the Worlds'.

PR: Great to talk Chris, and many thanks for sharing your thoughts and ideas with us.

CM: Thank you Peter. ●

IN THE NEXT ISSUE

*Enter the
ironic, quirky, and
thoroughly captivating
world of Mick Brownfield,
as one of the most
energetic, and eclectic
illustrators in the business
shares his thoughts
and experiences of life on
the deadline.*

*Plus a look at the life, times and career of Brian Sanders, the twin talents of
Anne and Janet Grahame Johnstone, and Derek Eyles action-packed art.*

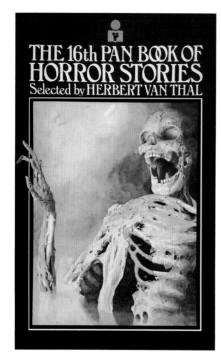

The Nightmare Painters

Johnny Mains draws back the shroud to reveal the stories behind the cover art for Herbert Van Thal's infamous Pan Book of Horror Stories.

ABOVE AND FACING PAGE:
One of the artists whose work came to the attention of David Larkin during his tenure at Pan Books was Alan Lee. A succession of darkly Gothic covers for Pan including 'Sir Arthur Conan Doyle's Tales of Terror and Mystery' and the covers to the 16th and 17th *Pan Book of Horror Stories* prompted Larkin to commission Lee along with friend and fellow fantasy artist Brian Froud, to collaborate on the best selling book 'Faeries', which propelled the work of both artists to an international audience.

THE PAN BOOK OF HORROR STORIES is the infamous, longest running horror anthology series that ran from 1959 until 1989. It was collated under the guidance of two editors: Herbert van Thal and, following van Thal's death, by Clarence Paget. It is widely accepted that the first fifteen books contained the best content, and the content of the last fifteen earned the series almost legendary status. In fact, you may well have been amongst the many children in the playground, huddled together, swapping gory tales in the form of beaten up copies pinched from older siblings. Over 600 stories by around 400 authors found their way into the series—and some of those made it to the top spot: the springboard for the cover of the book itself. Titles like 'The Squaw' by Bram Stoker; the iconic, snarling cat on the cover of Pan Horror 1, or the painting from *Pan Horror* 16 depicting Norman Kaufman's 'An Experiment with H2O'.

They say one should never judge a book by its cover, but if it wasn't for the cover art on *The Pan Book of Horror Stories*, these books may well have been less well regarded. A lot of the noise surrounding the series, like many other forms of entertainment at

the time (video nasties anyone?) came from people and parents who caught a startling glimpse at the covers, and failed to ever view the contents. The problem with the *Pan Horrors*, as far as *illustrators'* readers are concerned, is that a fair number of the covers were of the photographic variety. This move was the brain-child of David Larkin, art director at Pan, whose decision to move away from the traditional painted cover and into still life photography was a breakthrough for Pan, but for others it destroyed the brand.

The in-house photography department would borrow or buy most of the props from Bonham's—fine art auctioneers and valuers—and if the shots weren't taken in the studio, would take place in Richmond Park, where Pan employees enjoyed dressing up and running riot. Another move away from the traditional Pan style was the iconic yellow box—and getting rid of the many talented lettering artists (the technique faded out around 1969) in favour of hot metal type, photo-setting, and Letraset.

But for a while, and sometimes decades apart, the *Pan Horrors* were known for their painted covers; be it a beastie peeking out from under its tomb, spectres; some unfortunate's decapitation, or other gruesome and bold imaginings. And this is where you, the *illustrators'* reader may come in. I'll list who painted which cover as far as I'm able, but there are gaps in

ABOVE AND FACING PAGE:
The richness and variety of cover art to these pocket sized 'shockers' is seen to it's greatest effect from the anonymous first volume, where the malign feline from Bram Stoker's 'The Squaw' spits defiance, through to two takes on book 7 (the bats being another of Francis Phillipps' works) and the masterly and shudder inducing art of Alan Lee on the 17th volume.

knowledge—covers I've not been able to give an artist's name to. If the style looks familiar, please e-mail me.

Panned—The Fate Of The Pan Artworks

So what happened to the artwork after the series came to an end? This is where the story becomes rather sad. Two people enter the scene here: first Ken Hatherley, who worked in the art store, and the other, Colin Larkin who purchased a substantial part of the Pan Artwork Archive.

Ken was in charge of the art store, and it held around 5,000 original artworks in brown paper envelopes, with no filing system, and no real way to know what was there. The management at Pan didn't appear to value what they had: the art director, George Sharp, was alleged to have said that he'd happily burn the lot! Eventually, they employed Stan Boswara (who had recently retired from Pan) to try and track down as many of the artists as possible in order to return the pieces. He spent a year researching, and only succeeded in getting in touch with a couple of names. During this time,

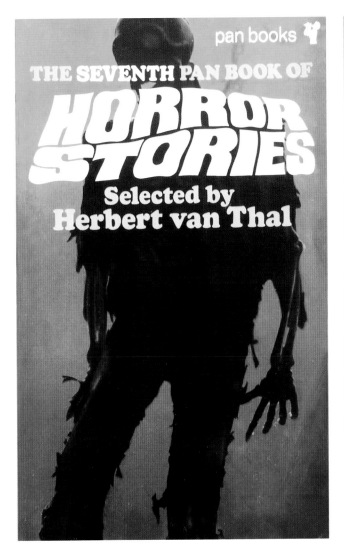

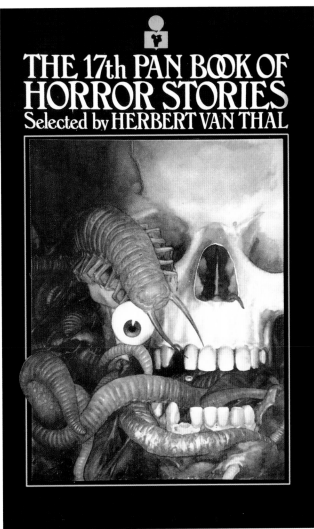

artwork was routinely being given to visitors, and those working in the building took pieces away. The adage was "If you like a picture, take it!"

Ken was made redundant soon after Stan was employed, and not long after that Pan Macmillan moved offices. But in days before he left Ken revealed that the carnage had started.

"The mail boys were coming into the art store and picking up armfuls and taking them outside and dumping them in skips".

And it turns out it wasn't just the artwork. One of the employees at the time took home two paintings from a skip, saying to her partner that she'd found them—did he know what they were? She also said that there were folders and folders of paper work. Her partner knew exactly what the artwork was—the second and seventh paintings to the Pan Book of Horror Stories. He raced round to the skip, which was at the back of Pan's old offices, but alas, it was gone. In my own researching into the Pan Horror history, I was told that everything pre-1987 simply

didn't exist anymore—all of that history, and probably not just for the Pan Horrors, but a major part of the Pan archive; letters, contracts... thrown into landfill and rotting...but some escaped.

Before he left, Ken got in touch with Colin Larkin, brother of the now ex art director Dave. Ken knew that Colin was a huge fan of the older Pan books, so much so that he made an offer of "£600.00 for two lots of 400(?) illustrations."

Colin said, "In 1990 I purchased directly from Pan Books a vast collection of original cover artwork, some 600 pieces. They ranged from 1947 through to the '70s, with the vast majority being from the Golden Age 1950 to 1966, when UK Paperback publishers attempted to copy the USA Pulp covers.

In 1991, for financial reasons, I was forced to auction part of this collection. The subsequent auction at Bonhams resulted in a considerable stir in the UK press, and on television. Some of the original artists created a flurry of activity by claiming that Pan Books had no right to have sold them to me. I was not

ABOVE: Such was the success of the *Pan Horror* series, that other collections were tried out by Pan, including two volumes devoted to adaptations of Hammer Horror films. This example shows Sam Peffer's original cover art for 'The Second Hammer Horror Omnibus'.
RIGHT: Josh Kirby's cover for the 13th volume.
FACING PAGE: Mel Grant's cover for the 30th, and last, book in the series.

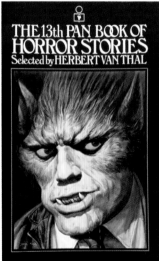

involved in any of the subsequent activities, and Pan Books were able to demonstrate that they did have 'good title' to sell the goods. A settlement was made to the artists in 1992, and everything was resolved."

But if Ken's original estimate of 5,000 artworks kept in the store is correct, that means around 4,000 pieces are unaccounted for. The artwork for 2 and 7 is in a private collection. I own the artwork to 3 (bought from a dealer who sourced it from the Bonhams W F Phillipps sale) and 16 (bought from a private collector). The artwork to 14) is in an American collection, mis-sold as a Dr Phibes artwork. I believe that Alan Lee still owns the artwork to 17. Peter Geissler owns the artwork to Pan Horror 24. The Steve Crisp artwork for Pan Horror 26 is in the collection of Jane Frank and the artwork for Pan Horror 30 is with its artist, Melvyn Grant.

Taking away the first volume, and the volumes with photographic covers—that still leaves a few pieces of artwork (including reprint covers) missing.

The Pan Book of Horror Stories has been a major part of my life since I first read volume 13 at the age of thirteen. Twenty-three years have passed, and this delightful series never fails to surprise and delight me. I hope that one by one, the lost pieces will stagger

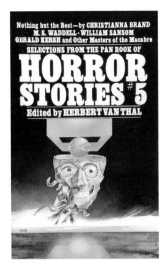

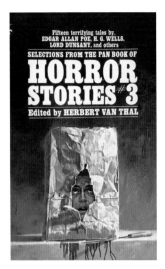

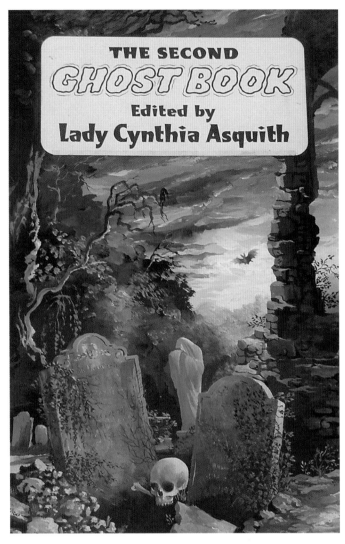

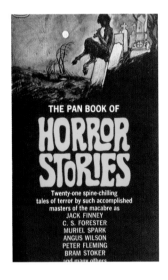

ABOVE: Covers to the US editions of the series published by Fawcett Gold Medal/ Berkley Medallion. The cover art veered towards the whimsical, rather than the gothic horror of it's UK progenitors, making for a very alternative take on the *Pan Horror* legacy.

ABOVE RIGHT: Pan also launched a companion series which eschewed gore in favour of the supernatural. Edited by Lady Cynthia Asquith, the *Pan Ghost Books* provided yet another source of short stories with a hint of unease as Val Biro's cover art so adroitly conveys.

home like a much maligned son, to wreak a horrible revenge. I hope so, because the alternative is a far more grisly end. ●

● Johnny Mains is an award winning editor, historian and author. Email him with any questions or even answers at: *panbookofhorrorstories@gmail.com* For more about the *Pan Book of Horror Stories* and it's editor Herbert van Thal a new book has been written by Johnny entitled 'Lest You Should Suffer Nightmares'. Available from Screaming Dreams at: *www.screamingdreams.com/nightmares.html*

Loathsome Listings

Pan Horror 1 – Unknown. Depicts a scene from Bram Stoker's 'The Squaw'. Reissue: Photo.

Pan Horror 2 – SR Boldero (1898-1987). Known mainly for his Pedigree and Arrow cover art, most notably Satanism and Witchcraft, Prince of Darkness, Not at Night. Reissue: Photo.

Pan Horror 3 – William Francis Phillipps (?-?). A prolific artist, of whom nearly nothing is known. Mainly painted for Pan, Penguin and New English Library, most famous for his *Edge* covers. He also painted many covers for the *House of Hammer* magazines. Reissue: Same cover used.

Pan Horror 4 – William Francis Phillipps - a cover which could just as easily been applied to Pan's *Ghost Stories* series. Reissue: Photo.

Pan Horror 5 – Photo (the skull part of this photo was also used on John Burke's Tales of Unease). Reissue: Same cover used Pan Horror.

Pan Horror 6 – William Francis Phillipps.

Pan Horror 7 – William Francis Phillipps. Depicts story from David Grant's 'The Bats'. Reissue: Unknown. Possibly depicts the climatic moment from W.W. Jacobs' 'The Monkey's Paw'.

Pan Horror 8 to 12 – All photo covers. No variant covers after *Pan Book of Horror Stories 8*.

Pan Horror 13 – Josh Kirby. (1928-2001) Forever linked to Terry Pratchett's Discworld series. Also painted the posters to Life of Brian and Return of the Jedi. The werewolf painting was originally commissioned for a *Men Only Magazine* editorial. It has since been used by a German publisher for the Carl Dreadstone novelisation of 'The Wolfman'.

Pan Horror 14 – Josh Kirby. Depicts Sir Gore Caruthers from Ron Chetwynd Hayes' 'It Came to Dinner'.

Pan Horror 15 – Unknown.

Pan Horror 16 – Alan Lee. Depicts Norman Kaufman's 'An Experiment with H20'.

Pan Horror 17 – Alan Lee (1947 -). Another artist linked with an established series, this time 'The Lord of the Rings'. Co-creator with fellow illustrator Brian Froud of the best selling 'Faeries' his paperback cover art includes, 'The Once and Future King' by T.H. White and Sir Arthur Conan Doyle's 'Tales of Terror and Mystery' (Pan).

Pan Horror 18 to 23 – All photo covers.

Pan Horror 24 – Peter Geissler. Commercial artist. First commission while in college was Pan Horror 24. Tried to achieve an airbrush effect with his painting. It was actually acrylic on board. Possibly commissioned by Gary Day Ellison. Now works with a 'major artist working in the South West'.

Pan Horror 25 – 'typographic' cover.

Pan Horror 26 – Steve Crisp (? -) Renowned illustrator. Known for his many Stephen King and Richard Laymon book covers. Has also designed many jigsaws. Depicts the story 'Flies' by John H. Snellings.

Pan Horror 27 – Stuart Bodek (?-?)South African artist who worked through Artist Partners. Depicts the story 'Pebbledene' by Alan Temperley. Is generally regarded at the most gruesome cover of the whole Pan series.

Pan Horror 28 and 29 – are photo covers.

Pan Horror 30 – Melvyn Grant (?) – Another artist forever linked with a series, this time Darren Shan's Demonata series. Has also painted many works for Iron Maiden, most notably 'Fear of the Dark'. Depicts the story 'The Lawnmower Man' by Stephen King.

Other Editions

There have been foreign reprints of the Pan Horrors—four US books and, one German. The US ones were published by Fawcett Gold Medal/ Berkley Medallion and were the 1st, 3rd, 4th and 5th volumes—although not all of the stories from the original volumes were published. The artists to these volumes are unknown; apart from volume 5 which is signed 'Valla'. Victor Valla is alive and well; an artist whose, sometimes complex work, has appeared on H. P. Lovecraft and Robert E. Howard books.

Reproduced by kind permission of the van I hal Estate

LEFT: Herbert Van Thal, editor and literary agent, whose name became synonymous with the series. It was Van Thal's devotion to the craft of the well honed short story, and enthusiastic mentoring of many an ingenue author (some were only recently out of school) that added so much colour and vitality to the series.

L. Ashwell Wood

Jeremy Briggs and Peter Richardson take a nostalgic look at the cutaway world of one of illustration's more unusual exponents.

THE WORK OF LESLIE ASHWELL WOOD is immediately familiar to anyone old enough to have grown up in post war Britain, and to have been one of the many millions of readers of the *Eagle*; the comic that embodied the spirit of optimism necessary to rise above the privations of austerity which still clung to the very fabric of 1950s Britain. Ashwell Wood's distinctive contribution was not however comics related, but it was every bit as compelling as 'Dan Dare' or 'Riders of the Range'. It was about as niche market as an illustrator's work can be, but was so universally compelling that he was guaranteed an audience for as long as he produced his own particular brand of illustration.

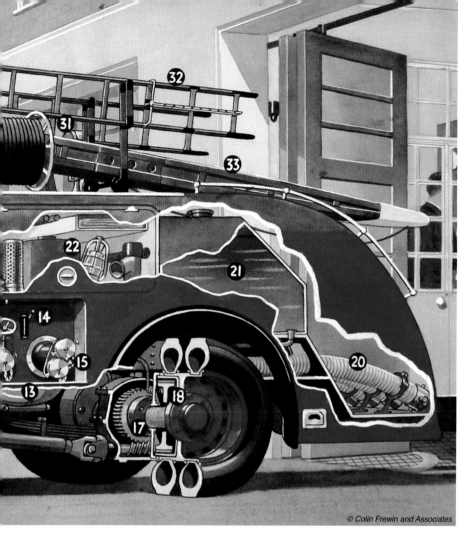

ABOVE: Leslie Ashwell Wood and his wife Florence, in coquettish mood, at a formal function in the 1950s, when the artist was at the height of his fame. His work at this stage of his career, was appearing every week in the best selling UK comic the *Eagle*, resulting in a following running into the millions.

ABOVE LEFT: Typical of the work that Leslie Ashwell Wood is so well remembered for, a fire engine from the centre-spread of *Eagle comic* in 1952.

LEFT: Another of Wood's *Eagle* cutaways—the cross-channel Hoverlloyd hovercraft, which commenced operations in 1966.

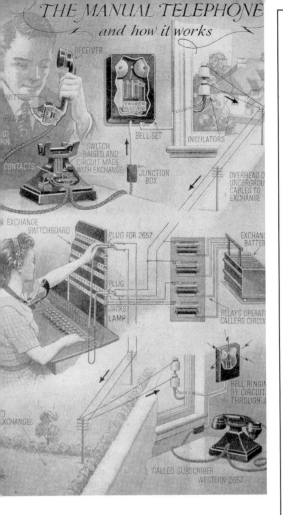

THE MANUAL TELEPHONE
and how it works

RECEIVER

TRANSMITTER

BELL SET

INSULATORS

CONTACTS

SWITCH RAISED AND CIRCUIT MADE WITH EXCHANGE

JUNCTION BOX

OVERHEAD O UNDERGROU CABLES TO EXCHANGE

EXCHANGE SWITCHBOARD

PLUG FOR 2657

EXCHAN BATTER

PLUG

JACKS LAMP

RELAYS OPERATI CALLERS CIRCUI

BELL RINGIN BY CIRCUIT THROUGH J

XCHANGES

CALLED SUBSCRIBER WESTERN 2657

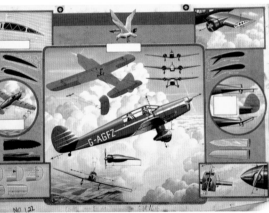

G-AGFZ

GIFTS FOR HOLIDAY MAKERS!— SEE INSIDE

The MODERN BOY 2D.

EVERY MONDAY.
Week Ending August 2nd, 1930.
No. 130.
Vol. 5.

TESTING THE LOCO'S HEART-BEATS.—*See page 3,*

ABOVE TOP: From the days when you were lucky if you even knew someone with a telephone; an illustration by Wood of 'The Manual Telephone' from Odhams *Modern Wonder* circa 1938/39.
ABOVE: Illustrations depicting wing and wing flap design.
ABOVE RIGHT: The August 2nd 1930 edition of *Modern Boy*, shows railway engineers testing a steam locomotive's "heart-beats".
FACING PAGE: The newly christened 'Duchess of Gloucester' as it appeared on the cover of *Modern Wonder* in 1938.

Leslie Ashwell Wood's speciality was the cutaway, and his work was so well informed, and so fascinating it would defy all but the most jaded of readers not to be drawn into his world.

Wood's background was, it appears, well suited to his passion for revealing the workings of mechanical marvels. Born in 1903, and exhibiting a passion for science and engineering as well as art, his subsequent career was not really that unpredictable, and in terms of timing, there couldn't have been a more auspicious moment for someone of his talents to embark on the world of work when he left full time education at beginning of the 1920s. An era where young people with drive and determination could gain worthwhile employment and build on their skills whilst working on the job rather than digging themselves into debt in the halls of academe. Although much of Wood's life remains shrouded in mystery, it appears that the experience that

ABOVE: One of Wood's working drawings form the 1930s, unveiling the mysteries of a 'Magic Lantern Show'.
FACING PAGE: Three more of Wood's covers for *Modern Wonder* where his ability to provide enticing colour, to add further clarity to his dissections of machinery, really came to the fore.

would serve him so well in his artistic career was gained at the premises of Fairey Aviation, at Hayes in West London. Fairey's speciality was in the design and production of naval aircraft, a relatively recent innovation, but one which would prove crucial some twenty years later when Britain was again plunged into war, and carrier-borne aircraft such as Fairey's Swordfish biplane bomber, were a vital part of the Royal Navy's arsenal. Wood's work at Fairey Aviation soon required him to devote his energies to preparing working drawings of every element that the company was fashioning for it's aircraft, and with the requirement for accuracy and clarity underscoring all of Wood's output, he rapidly absorbed all the disciplines that would later inform his illustration.

Whereas illustrators, with a traditional art college training, would make a guesstimate by eye when depicting an object, Wood's perception was shaped by the production process required of all technical draughtsmen engaged in the production of working drawings. This involved drawing the object from different angles, as well as an isometric projection from the calculations involved, to create a 3D impression on the page. No guesswork was involved,

and the whole process was firmly based on a thorough understanding of all the disciplines involved in technical drawing. It was precisely this highly demanding training that was to provide such authority and clarity to Wood's illustrative output when, seeking new outlets for his creative energies, he first began to submit his work for publication in the rapidly expanding field of technical, and educational magazine publication.

Wood's first published work appeared in the February 3rd 1933 issue of *The World Of Wonder*. The illustration, initialled "LW", had an immediate resonance with an audience enjoying the benefits of the mass electrification that was adding such impetus to twentieth century living. Entitled 'How The Dynamo Produces Electricity In Vast Quantities For Light And Power', the double page spread depicted a partial cutaway and exploded view of an industrial electrical generator. The magazine was one of what would become a succession of educational publications aimed at older children, published by the Amalgamated Press (AP), one of the UK's largest purveyors of periodicals. *The World Of Wonder* was edited by Charles Ray, and Wood's work was highly

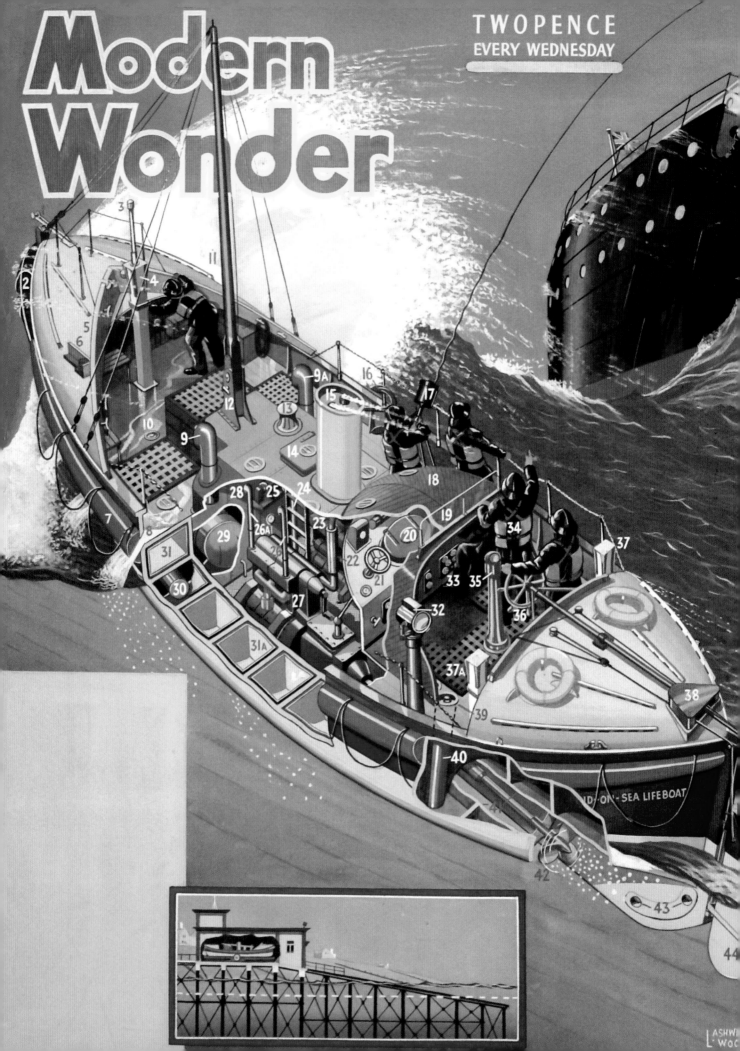

Modern Wonder

TWOPENCE
EVERY WEDNESDAY

---

regarded by Ray, who proceeded to keep him busy with furnishing artwork for *The World Of Wonder,* and a sister publication with an altogether more historical bias entitled *The Romance Of The Nation,* where Wood's cutaways depicted such subjects as siege machines from the middle ages and Tudor warships.

His work with Ray and AP continued apace, and he contributed to a succession of titles by Ray, including *The Popular Science Educator,* and the aptly titled *Everybody's Enquire Within.* However, as colour printing became less expensive, new opportunities for Wood to expand his repertoire presented themselves, and ever eager to avail himself of new challenges in 1937, he was able to add the prestigious publisher Odhams Press to his curriculum vitae. The title, *Modern Wonder,* was very reminiscent of the periodicals he had worked on with AP, but the addition of colour printing to both the cover and centre-spread enabled audiences to see Wood's work in colour, which not only greatly enhanced their attractiveness, but also added further clarity to Wood's revelatory artworks.

The next four years would see Wood as a regular contributor to *Modern Wonder,* but with the declaration of war in September 1939, and severe restrictions on the use of paper as the U-boat blockade began to bite, *Modern Wonder,* now re-titled *Modern World* was cancelled in March 1941. Wood's outlets were shaped more by events beyond his studio, rather than career moves made by the artist himself. The redirection of Wood's energies lay partly in his contribution to a succession of war orientated information books published by Odhams Press, which according with the spirit of the times, had such typically gung ho titles as; 'Britain's Wonderful Fighting Forces', 'Britain's

© IPC Media

FACING PAGE AND ABOVE:
Two more of Wood's covers for *Modern Wonder,* including an original painting of the workings of a lifeboat with lettering painted directly onto the illustration board, and the flight deck of an aircraft carrier; "Britain's New Wonder".

83

ABOVE: Leslie Ashwell Wood's artwork for the *Eagle*, propelled his illustrations into the consciousness of a new generation of readers, whose fathers may well have encountered his work in the pages of *Modern Wonder* and *Modern Boy* some twenty years earlier. The illustrations above are all sourced from the original paintings and depict a look at railways of the future ABOVE, and a breakdown crew ABOVE TOP, and a look at North American rail travel ABOVE RIGHT.

Modern Army', 'Britain's Glorious Navy' and 'Warfare Today'. A book entitled 'Britain's Merchant Navy' made special mention of Wood's contribution with the legend, "With more than forty explanatory drawings by L. Ashwell Wood."

Wood's work seems to have caught the attention of the Ministry of Information, and he produced a succession of artworks for training and civil defence purposes; several of which are held by the UK National Archives, as well as being available online at the National Archives as part of its 'The Art of War' exhibition.

As the war ended, and Britain entered its post-war recovery, the work that Wood produced for Odhams Press reflected a public appetite for a world beyond military concerns, and the publication of 'The Secrets of Other People's Jobs' began a run of work on less war-like books including 'Miracles of Invention and Discovery', 'Railways, Ships and Aeroplanes Illustrated', 'The World's Railways And How They Work', 'The Complete Book of Motor-cars, Railways, Ships and Aeroplanes', 'The World's Airways And How They Work', as well as several illustrations in the 1951 two volume set of 'Odhams History of the Second World War'. By this time however the next stage of Wood's career had begun.

In 1949, the unlikely combination of a jobbing commercial artist and a vicar, spawned what was to become a ground breaking comic, and as the Reverend Marcus Morris knocked on a succession of publishers doors with the carefully prepared dummy that he and artist, Frank Hampson had prepared, Leslie Ashwell Wood's career was due to enter its most fruitful

phase. When Hulton Press, finally made the call to Morris and the *Eagle* was launched in April of 1950, there was an immediate demand for work of a sufficiently wholesome and informative nature to reinforce Morris and Hampson's editorial remit that their publication should maintain the high standards they demanded for their youthful readership.

As a consequence, Wood's work was granted a prominent display on the centre-spread of each issue of the *Eagle* from issue 1 onwards. The commissioning of Wood seems to have occurred once the deal with Hulton had been cemented, as his work is absent from both the dummy issues that Hampson and Morris created. For the cost-conscious Morris this would have been a pragmatic move, Hampson's 'Dan Dare' was a strong enough concept to sell the project, the commissioning of other top-flight illustrators could wait until there was the strong financial backing that a publisher such as Hulton could provide. Once the call from the *Eagle* editorial team had been received, Wood's workload was as considerable as the demands of a weekly comic necessitated. His experience and stamina were such that he could meet the gruelling weekly deadlines, with very few breaks, when other artists would fill in. His schedule was maintained throughout the run, with no diminution of the detail and charm that he brought to each and every illustration he delivered to Marcus Morris' HQ.

A rare opportunity to see behind the wall of anonymity, which separated most illustrators from the public, presented itself as a result of Morris's enthusiasm for showing his youthful audience some of the procedures involved in publishing the *Eagle*. Under the banner 'How *Eagle* Is Produced',

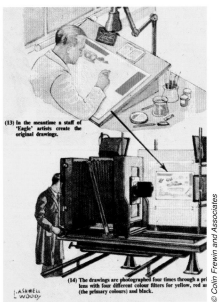

ABOVE: Wood makes a guest appearance in the feature; 'How *Eagle* is produced', where he depicts himself working at an angled drawing board in a white lab coat. Requisite wear for 'boffins', but an unlikely mode of attire for an artist working from home.

85

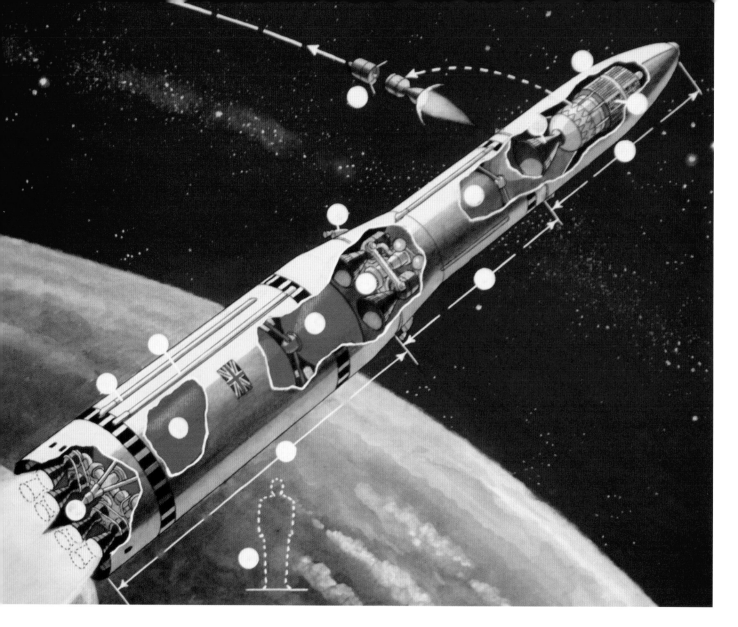

ABOVE AND FACING PAGE:
Satellite technology provided a very
fertile ground for Wood's talents
as these artworks from a 1962 copy
of Inside Information series reveal.

Wood produced a double page spread, which included a self portrait of
the artist working at an angled drawing board, supported on a table beside
a window with an Anglepoise lamp adding extra illumination. Elsewhere in the
comic there appears a photograph of Wood with the same artwork for 'How
Eagle Is Produced' in production. A couple more rare glimpses of the artist
appeared in the *Eagle*'s later years, but for the biographer Wood, frustratingly,
remains something of an enigma.

There was one tantalisingly brief interview that the *Eagle* conducted with
Wood and other commentators, which concerned the future of space travel
in early 1958. Whilst very little of Wood's contribution made it into print, the
transcript itself did survive, and was eventually published in the *Eagle Times*;
a small circulation journal which was avidly read by devotees of the *Eagle*. Only
a few months after Sputnik 1 was launched into orbit, and with the Apollo moon
landing over a decade into the future, Wood described the need to be factual
in his work, even when illustrating futuristic spacecraft by saying, "When I'm
drawing the pictures for the middle spread, I have to concentrate on known
research programmes. Personally, I think that the future of space travel, the
first journey to the moon, depends on the development of atomic power and
hydrogen energy." It is notable that Wood provided a cutaway of a scientifically

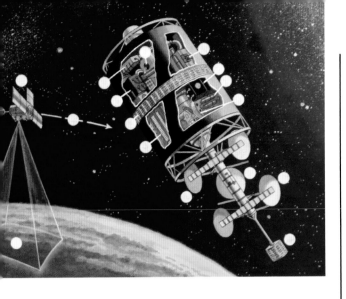

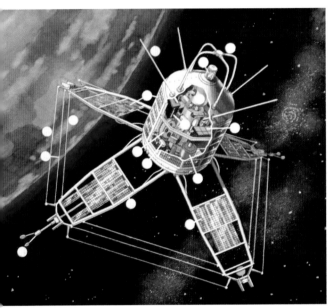

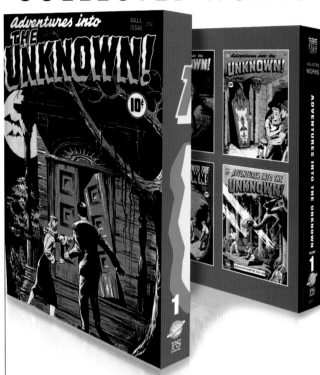

ABOVE: More of Leslie Ashwell Wood's paintings from the 'Inside Information' series. The book that these images appeared in explored the world of the hovercraft, which in 1971 was still a relatively novel means of water transport

realistic Earth-Mars spaceship for the 'Dan Dare Spacebook', published in 1953, which showed the craft containing an atomic reactor. He went on to say, "I'm sure that atomic power is the key to all our problems; not only space travel. We'll use it in time to power all transport, to activate agriculture in deserts and dustbowls, and even to eliminate disease. The harnessing of some of the unlimited resources of the mighty sea in the form of heavy hydrogen, which, with fusion, will provide heat and energy for countless years to come."

Wood's work was so highly regarded by the *Eagle* editorial team, that as well as being supplied with as much commissioned work as he could accommodate, he was also handsomely rewarded for his labours with one of the highest pay rates accorded the comic's freelance illustrators. In 1954, while other cutaway artists were paid around £30.00 to £35.00 per artwork, Wood received £42.00 per cutaway, and an additional £2.00 for illustrating a competition mini-feature. At a time when the national average wage was £8.00 per week, this equated to a very comfortable standard of living for Wood and his wife Florence.

With the merger of *Eagle* into the *Lion* comic in 1969, Wood's *Eagle* days came to an end, but this in turn led him in a new direction, when he commenced a series of 'informational' books under the imprint of Benwig Books. The books were in some respects a re-visitation to subjects already covered by his Eagle work but with the advantage of a more durable format

and for Wood himself, the satisfaction of seeing publications which were entirely devoted to presenting his work, rather than rubbing shoulders with a host of other contributors.

The books were published from 1969 through to 1971 under the banner of 'Inside Information' appearing in batches of four and were successful enough to see reprinting in both hard and soft-cover editions. Their bright and positive take on subjects such as transport, communications and space technology making them a firm favourite with young readers and their parents, not to mention librarians and teachers.

Sadly it was to be the last major project that the artist was involved in. Leslie Ashwell Wood died at the start of 1973 at the age of 69. He left behind a legacy of incredibly detailed cutaway drawings spanning five different decades, during which he produced upwards of one thousand cutaways on a multitude of different subjects. His *Eagle* cutaways are often quoted by former *Eagle* readers as being one of the highlights of the comic, and he is certainly best known for this work. As well as having examples of his artwork preserved in both the Victoria and Albert Museum, and the UK's National Archives, it is to his credit that some forty years after his death, his cutaways, no matter where they were printed, and whether they were aimed at children or adults, remain clearly understandable and accurate representations of their now historical subjects. In many ways he was one of the 20th century's least assuming, but most familiar chroniclers. ●

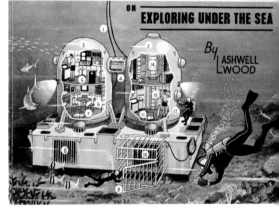

ABOVE: A typical cover from one of the 'Inside Information' books. Strong and simple, with his distinctive signature prominently displayed, the books provided Wood with a solo platform for his artwork for the first time in his long and distinguished career.

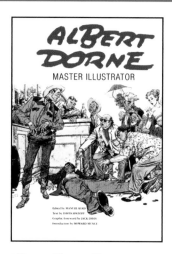

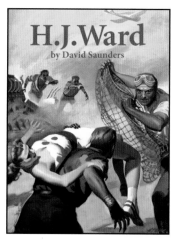

Albert Dorne Master Illustrator
by David Apatoff
Hard-bound 160 pages.
Auad Publishing £25.00/$34.95

DAVID APATOFF's 'Albert Dorne Master Illustrator' is a long overdue look at the work of one of America's premier league illustrators. A man whose work was once ubiquitous, and whose beetle browed visage would appear in ads for the *Famous Artists School,* which were published on a regular basis on the back of US comis in the early 1960s.

Dorne, in common with Robert Fawcett, also the subject of an earlier book by Apatoff, and also published by Auad, was more of a draughtsman than a painter, but his work was sublime, and in common with Fawcett, his drawing skill was ably abetted by his powers as a graphic storyteller, able to draw a viewer into a text with his powerful and dynamic compositions.

Apatoff's text provides an engaging biography, which recounts Dorne's career as an illustrator par excellence, along with his duties as one of the cofounders (Norman Rockwell being the other party) of the aforementioned Famous Artist's School.

The book is liberally illustrated with examples of Dorne's' work, as well as photos of the great man in his studio, and a heartwarming reminiscence by his daughter, Barbara Dorne Bullas.

Will Eisner's The Spirit–Artist's Edition
Edited by Scott Dunbier
Hard-bound 144 pages.
IDW £95.00/$125.00

IDW CONTINUE WITH THEIR monster sized 'Artist's Edition' series with the eagerly awaited 'The Spirit' volume.

Measuring a whopping 22 x 15 inches, this book is not something you will easily be curling up in bed with. As with all the previous volumes in this series, you have to prepare your reading ground carefully, but once you have removed the book from it's attractively designed outer packaging, you will find yourself experiencing the frisson of excitement generated when holding a page of original Spirit artwork in your trembling hand.

Because creating the sensation of holding original artwork in your hand is what this series of books delivers, and this volume is up there with the best of them. It's been eagerly anticipated for over a year now, and the wait has been well worth it, with 17 of the greatest Spirit stories beautifully reproduced, so every little bit of verisimilitude is lovingly reproduced, making this experience of reading Eisner's classic tales, unlike any previous encounter with these stories you might have had.

Buy now while stocks last, as the book already seems to be disappearing like the proverbial hot cakes.

H.J. Ward
by David Saunders.
Hard-bound 272 pages.
The Illustrated Press £29.99/$39.95

DAVID SAUNDERS' LOOK AT ONE of pulp art's most accomplished exponents, is a beautiful follow up to his earlier book on the life and work of his father, Norman Saunders'.

Like the previous volume, Saunders' Ward retrospective is a truly sumptuous blend of well researched biography and beautifully reproduced artwork, many sourced from Ward's surviving paintings which appear as bright and vital as the day he delivered them to his clients.

Ward's tragically truncated life is brought into full focus with the aid of Saunders' lively and engrossing text, coupled with photographs and letters, all of which help to add that extra dimension of accessibility to an artist whose work helped to define America between the prohibition years up until it's entry into the Second World War.

Ward's career was, in common with many of his contemporaries, effectively put on hold as his call-up papers carried him away from his studio and into uniform. The manner of his passing was particularly ironic, as it wasn't death in combat, but an undiagnosed cancer that wrote finis to an extraordinary output. Saunders' book is the ultimate testament to this great artist.

● *illustrators* is also available in the USA from **Budplant.com**
and in France from **Pulpsart.com** and **Album.fr**

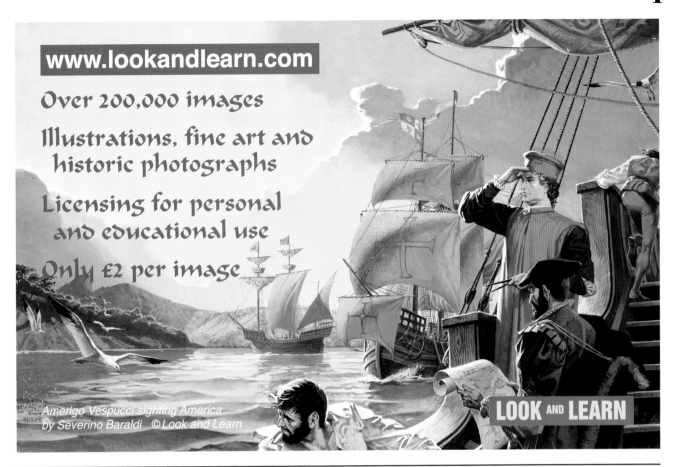

A feature on Graham Coton will be appearing in a forthcoming issue of illustrators.

The Studio Walter Wyles

Labels on image:
- Don Gilburn: Layout man
- Professional Models
- Philip Ashcroft: My Deputy
- Me
- Me
- Jean Hanlon: My secretary
- Jean Hanlon: My secretary
- Peter Read: Deputy Editor
- Joy Scully: Editor
- Barry Bourne: Deputy Picture Editor
- Wally's son Nick

ABOVE: Wyles had each of us photographed separately, and then made the composition for the opening spread from the individual photographs, which were taken in black and white. We were photographed in a variety of different poses: some of us were painted again as the smaller background figures, and we all featured in the background of the illustrations for subsequent installments.

ILLUSTRATOR WALTER (WALLY) WYLES loved painting watercolours of rumbustious Georgian scenes for women's magazine serials and book covers. He used professional models to portray the main characters, but preferred "real people" to model for the supporting characters. When I was art director of *Woman's Mirror*, a photogravure mass-selling woman's weekly magazine published in London in the sixties, I commissioned him to paint the illustrations for a romantic serial "The Passing of Paradise Row" by Paula Allardyce. Wyles decided that he wanted me, the editor Joy Scully, and some of the other staff to model for him. My secretary Jean Hanlon hired the photographer and photographic studio; hired all the period costumes, and ordered sandwiches, beer, and wine. Joy Scully, who was well upholstered, and a very good sport, modelled as a whore-house keeper, and I was a highwayman which, Scully told me, was a piece of excellent typecasting. It was a very enjoyable day, and the subsequent illustrations were stunning, and very lively! Wyles gave Joy Scully the original painting as a token of his regard for her. *Bryn Havord.* ●

WOMANS MIRROR 15 JUNE   20"   PAGES 6 & 7

**ABOVE: The finished painting as it appeared in the magazine, showing the crop marks and the printer's registration stickers.
LEFT: Walter Wyles working in the purpose-built studio in the grounds of his Jacobean farmhouse near Canterbury in Kent.**

● *A full feature about the works of Walter Wyles will be appearing in issue six of* **illustrators.**

In Passing The first in an occasional series of takes on illustration past and present.

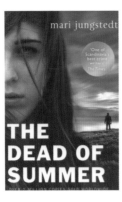
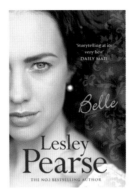
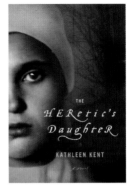
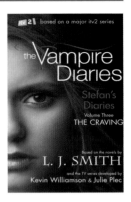

TODAY'S PAPERBACK ART DIRECTORS and art editors have a lot to answer for; or perhaps it's the marketing men and women. Since the 1970s, the trend has been to replace illustration with photography. I know from experience, that commissioning art work from illustrators is a highly skilled job, and I hear that there are not many art directors today who are possessed of the necessary skills. But that's no excuse! The examples show a variety of illustrated covers from the 1960s, contrasted with the ubiquitous 'half face' cover dominating some of today's output. Are they trying to bore their target readers into submission? The covers above patronise viewers with visual clichés, whereas the covers below invite the reader in with bold design and intrigue. Can publishers not bring back some visual excitement into our lives? *Bryn Havord.*●

Frank Bellamy's Heros the Spartan
Ltd (600) HC 272pp £95

Frank Bellamy's Heros the Spartan
Leather (120)
HC 296pp £265

Frank Bellamy's Complete Swift
LEATHER limited (200)
HC Slipcase 380pp £75

Frank Bellamy's Robin Hood
SC 144pp £14.99

Frank Bellamy's King Arthur and his Knights
SC 116pp £14.99

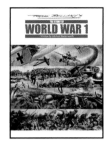

Frank Bellamy's Story of World War 1
limited edition of 200HC
112pp £25

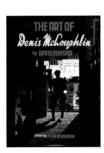

The Art of Denis McLoughlin
HC 272pp £45

Ron Embleton's Wulf the Briton
limited edition of 400
HC 352pp £125

Ron Embleton's Wulf the Briton
LEATHER limited edition
of 100HC 376pp £295

Karl the Viking
The complete collection
4 vol box set ltd 400
HC 520pp £159.99

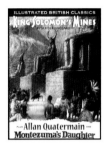

Illustrated British Classics King Solomon's Mines
SC 126pp £15.99

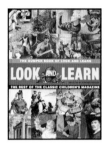

The Bumper Book of Look and Learn
HC 256pp £18.99

Eisner's Spirit Artist Ed
144pp HC £125

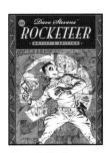

Steven's Rocketeer Artist Ed
36pp HC £95

EC's Mad Artist Ed
192pp HC £125

Kubert's Tarzan of the Apes
52pp HC £95

The Art of Bob Peak
HC 392pp £65

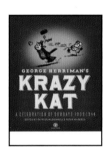

Krazy Kat A Celebration of Sundays
HC 160pp £85

Conan of Cimmeria Vol 1 Mark Schultz
480pp HC £130

Conan of Cimmeria Vol 2 Gary Gianni
384pp HC £130

Conan of Cimmeria Vol 3 Greg Manchess
416pp HC £130

Pandarve The Worlds of Don Lawrence
Ltd ed (250)
50pp HC £25

Albert Dorne Master Illustrator
160pp HC £29.99

Joseph Clement Coll The Art of Adventure
HC 168pp £35

All these books and many more are available from

Book Palace Books
www.bookpalacebooks.com
tel 020 8768 0022 (+44 20 8768 0022)
email: books@bookpalacebooks.com
FREE catalogue sent on request

Robert Crumb Sketchbooks 1982-2011
6 vol box set HC 1344pp £650 SALE £595

Letters

We received a lot of enthusiastic responses to our second issue of *illustrators*, but rather than hold back completion of issue three, we decided to publish your responses, comments, and suggestions in issue four. This means that comments on this issue will appear in issue six, but as you can see, we really appreciate all your feedback, and your letters add further insight into the appreciation of the artwork we feature.

I received my copy of *illustrators* two this morning, and I immediately stopped all work to read it. Once again, another great issue!

I knew about David Wright's Carol Day work, but his earlier work is very interesting.

And hey, my ad didn't look bad either!

I love Renato Fratini's work. I've known of his movie poster work, but his magazine and paperback work is fantastic.

Looking forward to issue three!

— **Mitch Itkowitz**

I've just received my copy of issue two of *illustrators* quarterly, and wanted to 'tip my hat' to a wonderful job. The feature on David Wright is absolutely fantastic, full of beautiful work from an artist I was only vaguely aware of, and all a working illustrator could need to get them inspired and at the drawing board. You'll be glad to know that I've posted a short feature on issue one on my web site at http://www.wingsart.net/home/2012/09/12/illustrators-magazine/ which I hope goes some way to help promote this excellent publication. I'll be sure to recommend issue 2 as well.

Many thanks to you and your team.

— **Christopher King**

Just got the second issue of your wonderful publication. It's packed with stuff!

I'm desperate to read...such talent.

Congratulations and thanks.

— **Mick Brownfield**

I want to thank and praise you and Geoff for the super article about my father and Carol Day. Patrick and I were talking about this yesterday and saying how much we owe to you, Geoff, and of course Roger Clarke for reviving interest in my father's work, it's lovely to think that he is out there in cyberspace for all to see. Also *illustrators* makes me realise just how talented and graceful my father's illustrations were (by the way, the two pencil drawings of the 'unknown model' were of my mother as well). Unfortunately all we thought about my father's efforts whilst we were growing up was that they put food on the table, and clothes for us to wear —with the odd Airfix kit thrown in. In fact I was more interested in his model aeroplanes than his strip cartoons when I was a child. When Patrick, and Nicky and I became adults, we were too busy with our own careers to fully appreciate who it was that gave us what talent we possess—as the Yanks would say "Was it ever thus".

Anyway I suspect that the disappearing reputation of my father's work has something to do with the fact that when he died, illustration in this country was considered 'trash'. I think that if he had been French and Carol Day had been Carol Jour, his memory and that of his creations would have been much higher—they do things better out there!

But now you and the others are correcting that, and both Patrick and I are very grateful.

— **Paul Wright**

It arrived today… the beautiful *illustrators*. Superb production. Wonderful… Congratulations to you all. I received number two. So after I have received number three I will subscribe asking you to include the first edition (number one and then number four) so that I don't miss any from the word GO. I love it ! Well done! I'm so proud to be included in a feature. Thank you!

— **Peter Maddocks**

I've received my subscriber's copy of *illustrators* two and again the quality is superb. The reproductions are wonderful, and you really have done justice to David Wright and Raymond Sheppard, as well as others in this issue. I hadn't realised that there were Amazon versions of the Carol Day strip available.

Seriously, you guys are doing such a fantastic job and I feel privileged to be involved in my small way.

— **Norman Boyd**

● *We really appreciate your help Norman!*

We are pleased to have your views about *illustrators*, so please write to the editor, Peter Richardson, at Illustrators. The Book Palace. Jubilee House. Bedwardine Road. Crystal Palace. LONDON. SE19 3AP, or e-mail him at <p-r@dircon.co.uk>